CHILD ANALYSIS TODAY

Child Analysis Today is one of a series of low-cost books under the title PSYCHOANALYTIC **ideas** which brings together the best of Public Lectures and other writings given by analysts of the British Psycho-Analytical Society on important psychoanalytic subjects.

The books can be ordered from:
Karnac Books
www.karnacbooks.com
Tel. +(0)20 8969 4454
Fax: +(0)20 8969 5585
E-mail: shop@karnacbooks.com

Other titles in the Psychoanalytic Ideas Series:

Shame and Jealousy: The Hidden Turmoils
Phil Mollon

Dreaming and Thinking
Rosine Jozef Perelberg (editor)

Spilt Milk: Perinatal Loss and Breakdown
Joan Raphael-Leff (editor)

Unconscious Phantasy
Riccardo Steiner (editor)

Psychosis (Madness)
Paul Williams (editor)

Adolescence
Inge Wise (editor)

CHILD ANALYSIS TODAY

Editor

Luis Rodríguez de la Sierra

Series Editors

Inge Wise and *Paul Williams*

KARNAC

LONDON   NEW YORK

First published in 2004 by
H. Karnac (Books) Ltd.
6 Pembroke Buildings, London NW10 6RE

British Library Cataloguing in Publication Data

A C.I.P. for this book is available from the British Library

ISBN 1 85575 325 1

Edited, typeset and produced by The Studio Publishing Services Ltd, Exeter EX4 8JN

Printed in Great Britain

10 9 8 7 6 5 4 3 2 1

www.karnacbooks.com

CONTENTS

ACKNOWLEDGEMENTS

I wish to express my gratitude to all those who have contributed with their advice, ideas, comments, suggestions, and support to *Child Analysis Today*: Inge Wise, Riccardo Steiner, Felicity Dirmeik, Alicia Etchegoyen, Judith Perle, Joan Schachter, Audrey Gavshon, Cecilia Walters, Pauline Cohen and Leena Häkkinen.

Luis Rodríguez de la Sierra
Editor

CONTRIBUTORS

Dr Robin Anderson is a training analyst in adult, child, and adolescent analysis at the Institute of Psychoanalysis, where he was also chairman of the Child and Adolescent Analysis Committee. He is a consultant child and adolescent psychiatrist, and since 1991 has been consultant psychiatrist at the Tavistock Clinic. Until 2000, he was the head of the Adolescent Department at the Tavistock Clinic. He retired from this post in 2003, but still continues to teach both trainees and staff there. He now concentrates on teaching and working in his private psychoanalytic practice. He has published papers on child, adolescent, and adult psychoanalysis and psychotherapy, and contributed numerous chapters to books. He has edited two books: *Clinical Lectures on Klein and Bion* and, with Anna Dartington, *Facing It Out: Clinical Perspectives on Adolescent Disturbance*. He is particularly interested in early object relationships and the way in which they manifest themselves in later life, especially during adolescence. He has applied this in working with suicidal young people. His interest also extends to the way in which psychoanalytic work with children contributes to adult analytic technique.

Dr A. H. Brafman is a psychoanalyst of adults and children. He worked for many years in the National Health Service (NHS) as a child and adolescent psychiatrist. He has been involved in teaching programmes for psychotherapists and he is now Honorary Senior Lecturer at University College London and works at the Psychotherapy Department of University College Hospital in London. He has previously published *Untying the Knot* (2001, Karnac) and *Can You Help Me? A Guide for Parents* (2004, Karnac).

Rose Edgcumbe, now deceased, was a member of the Association of Child Psychotherapists and the British Psycho-Analytical Society. After training with Anna Freud at the Hampstead Clinic she worked there in many capacities in treatment, training, and research, and in other clinics in this country and in Russia. She published numerous papers on child analysis and a book about Anna Freud´s work and ideas: *Anna Freud: A View of Development, Disturbance and Therapeutic Techniques*.

Edna O'Shaughnessy trained first as a child psychotherapist at the Tavistock Clinic and then as a psychoanalyst at the British Psychoanalytical Society, where she is a training and supervising analyst; she continues to be a supervisor also for the Child and Family Department of the Tavistock. For many years she worked in the Child Development Department at the London Institute of Education. Children, adolescents, and adults have been her patients. She has published many papers and contributed to various books.

Dr Luis Rodríguez de la Sierra, training analyst and child and adolescent analyst of the British Psychoanalytical Society, did his medical training in Barcelona. He qualified as a psychiatrist in Barcelona and London, where he also trained as a group psychotherapist. He worked for many years in the NHS and at the Anna Freud Centre, and now works at the London Clinic of Psycho-Analysis and in private practice. He lectures and teaches in this country and abroad, and has published papers on child analysis and drug addiction.

Anne-Marie Sandler was born in Geneva, studied with Jean Piaget, and was for a time his assistant. She then came to England, where she trained in child analysis with Anna Freud, going on to complete the adult training in the British Psychoanalytical Society, where she is a training and supervising analyst. She was formerly Director of the Anna Freud Centre. She has published a number of papers, and, in collaboration with Joseph Sandler, wrote a book, *Internal Objects Revisited*, published in 1998.

Introduction

Luis Rodríguez de la Sierra

"The memories of childhood
have no order, and no end"

Dylan Thomas

Child psychoanalysis, as a subspecialty of psychoanalysis, appeared on the scene approximately eighty years ago. Since then, many have been the arguments that child psychoanalysis has caused, and continues to cause, among the numerous psychoanalysts who have responded to the challenges presented by this fascinating branch of psychoanalysis. The contributions of the British Psychoanalytical Society to the welfare of children have been immense (Yorke, 1998). At the present day, the mention of child and adolescent psychoanalysis immediately conjures up three names: Anna Freud, Melanie Klein, and Donald Winnicott. However, the field is particularly dominated by the memory of the two formidable ladies and the memories attached to the famous "Controversial discussions" (King & Steiner, 1991), which took place between 1941 and 1945 in London. This is unfortunate, because Winnicott's contribution is as important as theirs.

Despite the major influence and encouragement of these three important figures, the majority of analysts in the British and other Psychoanalytical Societies prefer to restrict themselves to working with adults. Only a relatively small minority also train in child psychoanalysis while the rest neglects what can be considered as the gateway to application, observation, and research. However, there has been, in recent years, an increasing awareness, among various government and important international organizations, of what the three figures I have just named always knew: the importance of psychological issues in man's early development. What we become as adults originates in our earlier experiences in childhood. It is during those early years that emotions are very powerful while the capacity to understand them is, paradoxically, meagre. The child and the infant need help (as well as their parents and carers) in comprehending these strong emotions (as does the child within the regressed adult on the couch). Psychoanalysts try to accomplish this with the help of verbal interpretations as well as non-verbal, tacit ones. The latter are directed mostly at the infant, be it real or "within", in whom the organizing power of words is absent. When a small child comes to us running in the middle of the night, crying and telling us that "a monster is chasing me", and we realize that the child is afraid of his shadow, we must try (as parents and carers) to help the child to understand what his shadow is. Understanding the shadows in our unconscious is what we aim at in psychoanalysis. That many psychoanalysts, strangely interested in "validating" the unconscious, prefer the tools of research of academic psychology to the tools of research that child psychoanalysis offers is a very puzzling and contradictory thing. Both Sigmund and Anna Freud, as well as others, referred to it but we often tend to forget their thoughts on the subject. *Quo vadis psychoanalysis?* (Brenman Pick, 2000; Freud, A., 1969; Freud, 1917a, 1925e, 1937c; Gay, 1988; Green, 2000; Hellman, 1990; Jones, 1957; Steiner, 2000).

Although there have been many other important contributions to the field of child and adolescent analysis in this country (John Bowlby, Irma Brenman Pick, Dorothy Burlingham, Paula Heimann, Ilse Hellman, Susanna Isaacs-Elmhirst, Betty Joseph, Eglé and Moses Laufer, Anne Hayman, and Clifford Yorke, among others), the major differences in theory and clinical approach continue to bear the mark of Anna Freud, Melanie Klein, and Donald Winnicott.

The papers in this book provide an insight into the nature of these differences.

The book represents an attempt to portray the state of child psychoanalysis in the British Psychoanalytical Society today. It offers a variety of clinical and theoretical perspectives, and attempts to demonstrate how they influence the world of child psychoanalysis in this country. This divergence continues to divide psychoanalysts who think of early development and children's mental life differently and therefore approach their small patients in, at times, an entirely dissentient, technical way.

In spite of their common interest in child psychoanalysis and the fact that they were both pioneers in the field, Anna Freud and Melanie Klein did not join forces, and agreed on very little (Likierman, 1995). These differences are clearly illustrated by the papers of Edna O'Shaughnessy, Robin Anderson, Rose Edgcumbe, Luis Rodríguez de la Sierra, and Anne-Marie Sandler, who approach child analysis from a Kleinian (O'Shaughnessy and Anderson) and a Contemporary Freudian (Edgcumbe, Rodríguez de la Sierra, Anne-Marie Sandler) perspective. However, it must also be said that although Melanie Klein and Anna Freud articulated different, albeit very important, issues regarding child psychoanalysis and its status, their contribution has influenced every subsequent generation of child analysts in a way that is not always acknowledged by psychoanalysts sitting on opposite sides of the divide.

Winnicott's highly original contribution to child psychoanalysis has been enormous and has greatly influenced all child analysts after him. Abrahão Brafman's paper is written from an Independent, Winnicottian psychoanalytic perspective and offers us a clear idea of "another" way of looking at this fascinating but often-underrated field.

Melanie Klein's innovative and imaginative approach to the understanding of children took the field of child analysis by storm. She believed that the infant comes to this world with a readiness for social interactions and is therefore immediately capable of forming "object relations", even though these are rudimentary and incomplete. Melanie Klein suggested that the infant apprehends only "parts and portions of the object world" (Klein, 1935). The infant does react to maternal nurturing and becomes attached to a part of the mother that carries immediate significance for it, namely the feeding breast. Because the maternal feeding breast represents not only food but also offers comfort and pleasure, the infant identifies it as "good". The maternal breast, Klein says, can also be missed and when the infant is deprived of it, he then responds with frustrated aggression and consequently experiences it as "bad". On the basis of such beliefs, Klein hypothesized a rudimentary psychical activity existing from birth, which she called *phantasy*. According to Klein, such early *phantasy* gives form to infantile instinctual life and elaborates and represents worldly events internally, gradually enabling the emergence of clearer cognitive capacities in the infant. Melanie Klein envisaged a complex content to early *phantasy* and suggested that the infant could also use it for defensive purposes. Thus, overwhelming disturbance and anxiety in the infant trigger phantasies that reinforce a primitive mental mechanism of splitting of the object (not of the ego, as described by Sigmund Freud in "On fetishism", 1927e; "Splitting of the ego in the process of Defence", 1940e; and "An outline of psycho-analysis", 1940a). Klein felt that this helped to explain the mechanisms at work in adult psychiatric conditions and she concluded that all the important mental ingredients of adult psychotic illness are genetically present in early psychical life, and only become gradually harmless through healthy development.

To Anna Freud such advanced differentiating capacities in the infant were hardly credible. She clearly viewed their postulation as contrary to her father's developmental model, according to which the infant is initially sheltered in a foetus-like, primary narcissism. Freud saw the infant as noticing very little of the external world, his existence ruled by the pleasure principle and his primitive mind drifting into dream-like, hallucinatory states that hindered the full apprehension of worldly frustrations. Only gradually does the infant's mind accommodate the reality principle, and only then are object relations tenable. Anna Freud attributed the complex processes and pathologies, which Klein had situated very early in life, to much later stages of development. Having been a teacher, Anna Freud came to psychoanalysis equipped with extensive practical experience of the mind of the child, as well as an intuitive understanding of the way children think and feel, and understand the world. Not only was she well aware that children are intellectually and emotionally different from adults; she also knew how children greatly differ according to their age, as they move from one developmental phase to another. From this it follows that work with children requires a different approach from work with adults, whether that work be educational or therapeutic. From the very beginning, her psychoanalytic work with children was influenced by her detailed awareness of developmental issues. Whereas Klein focused on the early months of life for the origins of psychopathology, Anna Freud took into account developments extending throughout the years of childhood. Her focus on the Oedipus complex in the three- to five-year-old as the period during which the infantile neurosis is consolidated is often taken to mean that she discounted the importance of earlier disturbances. That this is far from true has been demonstrated by the views deriving from the war nursery observations she and her colleagues made at the then Hampstead Clinic, renamed The Anna Freud Centre after her death.

Klein and her followers extended the concept of phantasy to cover all forms of early thinking, as well as to describe unconscious mechanisms. In contrast, Anna Freud's work was moving in the opposite direction of distinguishing different forms of thought and fantasy, as well as defence mechanisms and other unconscious processes, from the content and processes of fantasizing. Melanie Klein's emphasis on the fantasy life of the child as centring on innate instinctual conflicts focused on internal objects led to a technique that emphasized early interpretation of primitive sexual and destructive wishes. To Anna Freud, the earlier form of conflict and anxiety is external, in which the child's immature ego is still siding with his wishes and impulses. Control depends on the child's objects and therefore he gets into battles with them over the satisfaction of his needs and wishes. This type of external conflict is considered infantile if it remains the dominant form (as in the case of delinquents) or if the child regresses to it at later stages (as in adolescence). While external conflicts are dominant, the child's anxieties are aroused by the external world. He fears, in sequence, the loss of the object (separation anxiety), loss of the object's love (after the establishment of object constancy),[1] criticism and punishment by the object (this becomes reinforced by the projection of his own aggression), and finally, castration anxiety. As the conflicts become internalized, they are now played out between his own ego/superego and id. In the Anna Freudian model internal conflicts are present very early on, but are independent from external pressures and lie between opposing trends such as passivity and activity, masculinity and femininity, love and hate. They are not conflictual early in life and become so only in the course of development, as the ego matures sufficiently for the development of the synthetic functions of the ego, which preside over integration, the process by which parts are combined into a whole. Klein was not impressed with this logic because for her the infant already begins life in a state of primary integration.

It is important to mention here how differently Melanie Klein and Anna Freud responded to Sigmund Freud's (1920g) theory of the life and death instincts, Eros and Thanatos. Klein used the death instinct as a clinical concept, the main cause of primitive anxiety in infants who fear destroying themselves or their objects. Anna Freud regarded it as a theory on the biological level and developed a theory of aggression more consonant with Freud's later ideas. She pursued the role of aggression within the context of structural theory, whereas Klein moved towards a theory of conflict between the instincts of life and death. Later on she introduced the concept of primary envy as a manifestation of the death instinct. To understand her ideas, we must remember that she placed the formation of the super-ego in the early months of life instead of the period between the third and fifth years. All this led to a very condensed view of development with little allowance made for cognitive development. As a result, similar interpretations of primitive sexual and aggressive wishes could be made to children and adults of all ages. For her, the child's experience of real people mostly served to correct the frightening internal fantasies and did not have, as Anna Freud maintained, primary importance in the development of patterns of relationships. Klein's view that what needed to be addressed were the innately given internal relationships between self and objects meant that she expected the transference of these relationships on to the analyst to be similar in children and in adults, leading to an emphasis on transference interpretation in both child and adult analysis. Anna Freud disagreed profoundly with all these views on the basis of her meticulous observations and experience of children in situations that grossly interfered with their real relationships to their parents. To Melanie Klein's assertions, she responded with the famous phrase: "The child is not, like the adult, ready to produce a new edition of his love-relationships, because, as one might say, the old edition is not yet exhausted."

Such different theoretical views of necessity gave rise to very dissimilar technical approaches. While Klein did not see much need for a different method with children and took it for granted, unlike Anna Freud, that playing was synonymous with adult free association, Anna Freud gave reasons for the need for a different technique. Children, she stated, do not usually and willingly present themselves in the analytic consulting room to be analysed; neither are they asked for their consent, nor do they know anything about psychoanalysis. They lack insight into their condition, make no voluntary decision to come into analysis, and do not particularly express a wish to be cured. They are taken up, most of the time, with the present, and the past in comparison holds little interest for them. In the ideal and desirable situation, the adult patient allies himself with the analyst of his own free will against a part of himself, of his own inner being. Such state of affairs is, of course, never or very rarely found in young children.

Although I have already noted that Anna Freud did not believe that the transference of children was the same as that of adults, I would like to repeat her reasons because this is, perhaps, the most important difference, in her opinion, between the analysis of children and the analysis of adults. The analysis of a child is not an entirely private affair because the relevant external objects still play an important role in the life of the child and, by extension, in the analysis itself. Children's real, age-appropriate, and normal dependence on their real, external parents is quite different from the adult's internal dependence on his fantasy parents. To Anna Freud, the question of whether children were able to develop a full transference neurosis was obscured by two of the peculiarities of child analysis: without the use of free associations not all the evidence for the child's transference appear in the material; and owing to the child's acting instead of associating, the aggressive transference is overemphasized and overshadows the libidinal one (Freud, A., 1965, p. 39).

Winnicott qualified as a child analyst in 1936 and had Nina Searl, Melanie Klein, and Melitta Schmideberg as his supervisors. He became a member of the British Society and then had a second analysis with Joan Rivière (his first analyst had been James Strachey). By the time the "controversial discussions" took place, he was considered a Kleinian. With his years of experience as a paediatrician, he was an important addition to Melanie Klein's group and she in fact named him as a Kleinian training analyst. But Winnicott was an individualist. He emphasized the role of the environment and the effects of experiences in early relationships and by 1951 he was no longer referred to as a Kleinian and Anna Freud gradually became more interested in his ideas, which she found more congenial. By this time, Winnicott was considered an important member of the Independent or Middle Group of the British Psychoanalytical Society. The influence of the environment in children's development plays an important part in Winnicott's approach to child analysis, a fact that distanced him from the Kleinian school and made him accessible and appealing to Anna Freud and her disciples.

Winnicott postulated that the phase between subjective infancy [in which even the maternal breast is experienced by the infant as an extension of the self] and the more objective perceptions of childhood might be the source of a variety of later attitudes. He was the first to describe the so called *transitional object*, an important concept applied to the rags, dolls, teddy-bears, and other objects that offer the child his first "not-me" experience. He was not, though, the first to observe such phenomenon, already described by Wulff (1946) and referred to as the *"talisman"* by Anna Freud (Freud, A., 1965). The transitional object is a possession. It is not an internal object such as described by Klein (which is a mental concept) nor is it (for the child) an external object as referred to by Anna Freud when talking about the vicissitudes of object relations and the way they develop through a gradual process of internalization that culminates with the resolution of the Oedipus complex and the formation of the super-ego. To Winnicott, the infant can use a transitional object when the internal object is alive and real and good enough (not persecutory). However, this internal object depends for its qualities on the existence, aliveness, and behaviour of the external object. Failure of the latter in some essential function indirectly leads to deadness or to a persecutory quality of the internal object. If the external object is persistently inadequate, the internal object fails to have meaning for the infant, and only then does the transitional object become meaningless too. The transitional object may therefore stand for the "external" breast, but *indirectly* through standing for an "internal" breast. The transitional object is never under magical control like the internal object, nor is it outside control as the real mother is (Winnicott, 1974, p. 11). The transitional object is an important developmental concept for Winnicott who regards it as helping the child to make the transition from infantile narcissism to object-love and therefore from dependence to self-reliance.

Another important Winnicottian concept is that of the *good enough mother*, which refers to the technique of mothering. When he says that the first object is the breast, the word "breast" is used to stand for the technique of mothering as well as for the actual flesh. Thus it is equally possible for a mother to be a "good enough" mother with a bottle as it is for her to be a "good enough" mother with her real breast of flesh. The good-enough mother is not necessarily the infant's own mother, but one who makes active and almost complete adaptation to the infant's needs, and as time proceeds she adapts less and less completely, gradually, according to the infant's growing ability to deal with her failure and to tolerate the results of frustration.

Playing has an important place in Winnicott's models of development and psychoanalytic technique. According to him, child analysis takes place in the overlap of two areas of playing, that of the patient and that of the analyst. Child analysis is about two people playing together. The corollary of this is that where playing is not possible then the analyst's work is directed at moving his patient from a state of not being able to play into a state of being able to play (Winnicott, 1974, p. 44).

There is no point in denying that, in spite of the efforts made by all child analysts in the British Society to find a common language and to reach mutual respect and understanding, significant differences of view remain. They exist alongside a wish to understand the disagreements, including knowledge from other sources. The importance attributed, clinically and theoretically, to the external and internal worlds of children; the recognition of developmental help as a legitimate psychoanalytic tool; early child development; and the meaning of play in child analysis are all concepts that are used and understood differently by many child analysts. Such variety of opinions needs to be taken into account if the reader is to understand the diverse ideas and techniques described in the papers included in this book.

While it is true that the various approaches used in these papers sound different, a parallel with the use of languages in the external world could be drawn. The same concept, psychoanalytic or not, may sound dissimilar when it is expressed in several languages precisely because it is being presented distinctively. In some languages part of the nuances of the same meaning will be lost, even though the essence would remain. When I refer to languages, I mean both the many tongues that exist in the world, and the specific languages of psychoanalysis (both the clinical and the theoretical languages) used by diverse psychoanalytic schools. No one has described this better than Balint (1968, pp. 92–116). It is a fact that patients improve with interpretations conveyed to them by their analysts in the analyst's own mother tongue (namely the language of the particular theoretical orientation of the analyst). Were we to accept this fact perhaps it would be then about time for psychoanalysts to consider the possibility that the supremacy of the interpretation *per se* might be nothing more than a Utopia, and entertain the idea that although interpreting plays a very important role in psychoanalysis, it may be a transitional role with a transitional value as opposed to a final and definitive one.

Nowadays all child analysts, irrespective of their psychoanalytic mother tongue, have moved towards less extreme positions and there is a clearly discernible effort to apply and develop the original findings of the three pioneers. Recent years have seen the convergence of research work by developmental psychologists, paediatricians, and neuro-scientists with psychoanalytic observations. Child analysts from different theoretical backgrounds have been able to exchange ideas and work together. This has influenced the way in which all child analysts approach, clinically and theoretically, the significance of both the external and internal worlds of children. Different approaches remain, although they are no longer always seen as mutually exclusive but as complementary. In each of the papers in this book there is clearly an analyst at work trying to make sense of the intricate and complex realm of childhood. The clashes and disputes present in the history of child psychoanalysis have not completely disappeared, but intimations of a wish to find a common ground seems to have, finally, started to emerge. I hope this book succeeds in revealing it to the reader.

Note

1. The establishment of object constancy enables a positive inner image of the object to be maintained, irrespective of either satisfactions or dissatisfactions. It is a pivotal stage for the whole future development of relationships. Without the capacity for object constancy, the individual will never achieve the ability to make and maintain reciprocal relationships which can survive disappointments, disillusionments, or frustrations, and within which he can willingly care for the object as well as demanding to be cared for. It is a very important concept at the moment of assessing suitability for analysis as it indicates the capacity to develop a transference and withstand the frustrations and restrictions of wish fulfilment of the analytic situation. It is painfully disturbed in cases of alcohol and drug addiction, as well as in delinquency, although the two conditions are by no means similar, contrary to popular belief.

References

Balint, M. (1968). *The Basic Fault: Therapeutic Aspects of Regression*. London: Tavistock.

Brenman Pick, I. (2000). Discussion (III). In: J. Sandler, A.-M. Sandler, & R. Davies (Eds.), *Clinical and Observational Psychoanalytic Research: Roots of a Controversy—André Green & Daniel Stern* (pp. 108–118). London: Karnac.

Edgcumbe, R. (2000). *Anna Freud: A View of Development, Disturbance and Therapeutic Techniques*. London: Routledge.

Freud, A. (1965)[1973]. *Normality and Pathology in Childhood: Assessments of Development*. Penguin University Books.

Freud, A. (1969)[1972]. Difficulties in the path of psychoanalysis: a confrontation of past with present Viewpoints. In: *Problems of Psychoanalytic Technique and Theory 1966–1970* (pp. 124–156). London: Hogarth Press.

Freud, A. (1971). The ideal psychoanalytic Institute: a Utopia. In: *The Writings of Anna Freud, Volume 7: Problems of Psychoanalytic Training, Diagnosis, and the Technique of Therapy 1966–1970* (pp. 73–93). New York: International Universities Press.

Freud, A. A short history of child analysis. (1966)[1971]. In: *The Writings of Anna Freud, Vol. 7: Problems of Psychoanalytic Training, Diagnosis, and the Technique of Therapy 1966–1970* (pp. 48–58). New York: International Universities Press.

Freud, S (1917a). A difficulty in the path of psycho-analysis. *S.E., XVII:* 137. London: Hogarth Press.

Freud, S. (1920g). Beyond the pleasure principle. *S.E., XVIII:* 7–64. London: Hogarth Press.

Freud, S. (1925e). The resistances to psycho-analysis. *S.E., XIX:* 211–222. London: Hogarth Press.

Freud, S., (1937c). Analysis terminable and interminable. S.E., *XXIII:* 209–253. London: Hogarth Press.

Freud, S. (1927e). On fetishism. *S.E., XXI:* 147–157. London: Hogarth Press.

Freud, S. (1940a). An outline of psycho-analysis. *S.E., XXIII:* 139–207. London: Hogarth Press.

Freud, S. (1940e). Splitting of the ego in the process of defence. *S.E., XXIII:* 271–278. London: Hogarth Press.

Gay, P. (1988). *FREUD: A Life For Our Time* (p. 523). London: J. M. Dent & Sons.

Green, A. (2000). What kind of research for psychoanalysis? In: J. Sandler, A.-M. Sandler, and R. Davies (Eds.), *Clinical and Observational Psychoanalytic Research: Roots of a Controversy—André Green & Daniel Stern* (pp. 21–26). Response to Robert S. Wallerstein, (pp. 32–37), Science and science fiction in infant research. In: J. Sandler, A.-M. Sandler, and R. Davies (Eds.), *Clinical and Observational Psychoanalytic Research: Roots of a Controversy—André Green & Daniel Stern* (pp. 41–72). London: Karnac.

Hellman, I. (1990). Research in a child guidance clinic. In *From War Babies to Grandmothers* (pp. 165–185). London: The Institute of Psycho-analysis and Karnac Books.

Jones, E. (1957). *Sigmund Freud: Life and Work,* Vol. II, p. 418, London: Hogarth Press

King, P., & Steiner, R. (Eds.) (1991). *The Freud-Klein Controversies 1941–45,* London and New York: Tavistock/Routledge.

Klein, M. (1935)[1981]. A contribution to the psychogenesis of manic-depressive states. In: *The Writings of Melanie Klein, Volume 1* (pp. 262–289). Hogarth and Institute of Psychoanalysis.

Likierman, M. (1995). The debate between Anna Freud and Melanie Klein: an historical survey. *Journal of Child Psychotherapy, 21*(3).

Steiner, R. (2000). Introduction. In: J. Sandler, A.-M. Sandler, & R. Davies (Eds.), *Clinical and Observational Psychoanalytic Research: Roots of a Controversy—André Green & Daniel Stern* (pp. 1–17). London: Karnac.

Thomas, D. (1953). Reminiscences of childhood. BBC Home Service Radio Programme, 6 May.

Winnicott, D. W. (1949). *The Ordinary Devoted Mother and her Baby*. London: Tavistock Publications.

Winnicott, D. W. (1953). Transitional objects and transitional phenomena: a study of the first not-me possession. *International Journal of Psycho-Analysis, 34*: 89–97.

Winnicott, D. W. (1964). *The Child, the Family and the Outside World*. Harmondsworth: Penguin.

Winnicott, D. W. (1971). *Playing and Reality*. London: Tavistock [reprinted London: Pelican Books, 1974].

Wulff, M. (1946). Fetishism and object choice in early childhood. *Psychoanalytical Quarterly, 15*: 450–471.

Yorke, C. (1998). Some contributions of the British Psycho-Analytical Society to the welfare of children. *The British Psycho-Analytical Society Bulletin, 35*(8): 1999.

CHAPTER ONE

Developments in technique in Kleinian child psychoanalysis

Robin Anderson

I t is now nearly ninety years since Melanie Klein first psycho-analysed a child, which led her to develop her special technique for analysing children. What is the Kleinian position now with regard to child analysis? Why and in what way does it differ from the technique originally described by her and restated by her in "The psycho-analytic play technique" (Klein, 1955)? In this chapter I look at Melanie Klein's technique of child psychoanalysis as it is practised now and consider some of the background to the changes in technique which have come about.

At first intuitively, but later relying on clinically based conclusions, Klein took the view that child psychoanalysis was psychoanalysis in its fullest meaning, not a mere application of psychoanalytic techniques. Klein felt that any modifications of technique should therefore only take account of the different means by which children communicate with the analyst, i.e. through various kinds of play as well as the usual free association and dreams as in adult analysis. Klein found that despite their immaturity and limited capacity to express themselves verbally, children could form the essentials of an analytic relationship: the capacity to form a transference relationship, communicate unconscious information to the analyst, to process interpretations, and develop insight. She realized this once she had discovered that children's capacity to play fills the gap left by their inability to follow Freud's analytic rule of free association. This was refined into her concept of "play technique". To have an analysis, children require a setting that provides them with the means of communicating with the analyst: a playroom with suitable toys, and an analyst willing to accept the child's need to be mobile and to engage in various play activities, including those that involve the analyst.

Klein found that children form an intense transference relationship with the analyst irrespective of their intense relationship with their parents. They form this early, and it is through the interpretation of the transference that the child's anxieties decrease. She felt that the most important task for children in their development was the mastering of anxiety. This fundamental task underlies the capacity to manage all the other developmental tasks, such as dealing with the Oedipus complex. She found that children have to cope with more anxiety than adults and yet have less developed and less mature capacities to do so. She believed very strongly that the direct and deep interpretation of anxiety, describing their unconscious fantasies, most effectively relieves children's anxiety. She felt it important to interpret the negative transference, though she felt this should always be in the context of a positive transference that was best established by interpretation and not by extra-analytic means. Klein's writing abounds with examples of her technique with children (see especially *The Psychoanalysis of Children*, 1975a, and *The Narrative of a Child Analysis*, 1975b).

In "The psycho-analytic play technique" Klein states:

> ... my work with both children and adults, and my contributions to psycho-analytic theory as a whole, derive ultimately from the play technique evolved with young children. I do not mean by this that my later work was a direct application of the play technique; but the insight that I gained into early development, into unconscious processes, and into the nature of the interpretations by which the unconscious can be approached, has been of far-reaching influence on the work I have done with older children and adults. [1955, p. 122]

Thus, child analysis made possible new discoveries about the mind that benefited psychoanalysis in general and, for a period after the Second World War, it was regarded as the pace setter in developments in Kleinian psychoanalytic technique. However, in the past thirty years this situation has changed: the most important contributions from Kleinian psychoanalysts have come from their work with adult patients, and these discoveries have in turn led to changes in technique. Kleinian child psychoanalysts have been heavily influenced by these changes in the technique of adult analysis.

The psychoanalytic setting

In all the basic physical and psychological settings, modern Kleinian child analysts follow Klein's basic guidelines more or less unchanged. The room is simple, with furnishings that are as far as possible robust, and surfaces that are easily cleaned. This leaves the child free to play in as unrestricted a way as possible without the analyst having to intervene too much to protect the room (as well as, of course, the child and the analyst). The room is devoid of materials belonging to other children, which again would require the analyst to intervene, though Klein did encourage other children's toys to be kept in locked drawers, a fact that would give some reality to fantasies about the existence of other child patients, which in turn would have links with fantasies about siblings and mothers' babies.

The toys should be small and simple to allow the child's own fantasy to be expressed in the play rather than the toys themselves suggesting too many fantasies to the child. The fact that each child has his or her own set of toys, which are kept in a locker or drawer, encourages a sense of continuity between the play in separate sessions. It also makes an analogy between the idea of an internal world containing internal objects, and the box or drawer containing the child's toys.

A boy of four in analysis because of disturbance arising from serious illness in his family systematically broke his toys into tiny pieces and tried to flush them down the sink. It seemed that this was an expression of his desperate wish to rid his mind of all ideas because their presence provoked distressing and disturbing feelings about his family. He was able to convey by his actions that he wanted his mind to be quite empty. Later, when he began to recover, his toys once more became a means of playing and expressing himself symbolically in a more peaceful way.

Frequency of sessions

In child psychoanalysis there are generally four or five sessions per week, to allow close contact and effective analysis. However, Melanie Klein did acknowledge to Esther Bick when she was developing the child psychotherapy training at the Tavistock Clinic that children do develop transference, which can be worked with analytically, even if they are seen only once a week. Nowadays, we would describe this as psychoanalytic psychotherapy rather than psychoanalysis, although the technique is very similar.

Parents

The analyst's relationship with the parents and their place in the analysis of their child is very important. As far as work within the sessions themselves is concerned, a child's comments about its parents would be considered like any other communication, much as an adult patient's references to their spouse would be analysed. Of course, a child depends on the parents to allow the analysis to take place, and often uses them to carry part of himself as, for example, when the child does not wish to come for sessions, leaving the parents to carry the motivation for analysis against which the child may vigorously protest. It is very important that these splits are fully analysed, particularly when they relate to negative transference, to avoid the parents carrying negative feelings of the child, which belong in the analysis. The parents must be regarded as the analyst's allies and it is important for both patient and analyst that contact is maintained. The usual arrangement would be to meet once per term, with an understanding that other contact, usually by telephone, would be made when necessary.

The problem of the parental contribution to the child's disturbance would not be regarded as something the analyst could or should attempt to influence directly. Of course, understanding the impact of this on the child, and managing the parents' transference to the analyst, can make a positive contribution to the parents as well as helping their child, but if this is not sufficient then the solution would be to seek additional help for the parents from elsewhere, leaving the analyst as free as possible to engage with the child. However, the management (rather than the analysis) of the relationship is crucial and the analyst does need to consider privately the nature of the relationship the parents have with the analyst.

Transference and interpretation

These two categories are considered together because how we understand the transference so much influences how we interpret to the patient.

Elizabeth Spillius (1983, 1988) has described how Kleinian technique in adult analysis had changed in the preceding thirty years, and noted the following four trends.

1. Destructiveness is being interpreted in a more balanced and less forceful way.
2. The use of part-object language describing the bodily expression of unconscious phantasy has been approached differently due to a shift of emphasis towards a greater interest in how part-objects function in the mind. In other words while the anatomical process—"You are putting your faeces into me" or "You experience me as a good feeding breast"—are present as ideas/hypotheses in the analyst's mind, he is much more likely to talk about what the patient is doing or experiencing in terms of the patient's conscious language. For example: "You are trying to relieve yourself by filling me with your confusion", or "You feel I have become more benign and helpful to you." The analyst may go on to connect this with the anatomical part-object processes, although often does not do so. This is described by Edna O'Shaughnessy as a concern with *psychological* rather than *anatomical* part-objects.
3. The concept of projective identification is being used more directly in analysing the transference and counter-transference.

4. As a result, there has been an increasing emphasis on acting in the transference and on the pressure experienced by the analyst to join in.

Spillius (1983, 1988) sees these changes as arising from several causes:

1. Bion's understanding of projective identification as a normal process of infancy and its use as a fundamental form of communication between infant and mother, patient and analyst.
2. Rosenfeld's development of this approach.
3. Betty Joseph's emphasis on the total transference situation and the way analysts can be powerfully drawn into subtle unconscious collusions with the patient.

I would add Hanna Segal's detailed work on symbolic functioning to the list.

Child analysts have been heavily affected by these changes, particularly in relation to methods of interpreting to children. Since they address the very fundamentals of the analytic relationship, which we hold applies just as fully to children as to adults, perhaps this is not surprising.

Analysing children places special demands on the analyst, demands that in many ways are more extreme than those which relate to most adult patients. It is often necessary to be able to process complex material quickly—to interpret under fire, to use Bion's phrase. To do this, the analyst is required, often very rapidly, to observe manifest behaviour, to consider personal feelings and their possible relevance to the child's behaviour, to come to a view about the underlying meaning of this in the child, and to respond by interpretation, sometimes at the same time as physically restraining the child.

If these pressures can be withstood and the analyst is able to remain open to the patient's projections and their meaning, as well as other material, it is possible to build up a three-dimensional picture of the object relationships of the child's internal world. Interpretations must take this into account since an interpretation is an action. If its potential meaning to the patient has not been understood, then the patient may experience it not as understanding but rather as some kind of enactment of an existing unconscious constellation. Another way of putting this is that we must consider who we are in the transference and whom the patient experiences the interpretation as coming from. These kinds of states are prominent in the paranoid–schizoid position and rapid fluctuations between paranoid–schizoid and depressive levels of functioning during a single session are relatively common.

I would like to illustrate some of these issues by presenting some material from an analytic session of an eight-year-old boy. This boy, whom I will call John, is the same child that I described earlier as destroying his toys. John had come to analysis at the age of four because, following the serious illness of a much loved older brother, he had become very angry and negative and had given up all positive aspects of his emotional and cognitive development. This included giving up all play. After entering analysis there were some distinct improvements, but he then became very negative again and I had noticed myself becoming very demoralized and rather weak with him. In exploring the possible meaning of my counter-transference at that time, I had concluded that what had been enacted between us and within me was a projection of a total transference situation, which was closely related to the crisis that had initially brought him to analysis. Something anti-developmental, which had led him to give up on himself and his creative development, had happened when he felt so despairing about the affliction of his brother. It was as though he had equated his illness with the triumph of hate over love. I thought that this despair had now lodged itself in me and that I had to struggle to deal with this first by understanding it and then interpreting, rather than by enacting the situation with him.

Once I had understood this and managed to strengthen my work with him, John seemed to come back to life and, although there were fluctuations in the quality of contact, there was a more hopeful and lively atmosphere. He was intermittently able to use the toys and to play, although at other times he engaged in a high degree of enactment with me. At times he resembled a child playing like an adult and free associating. At other times he was much more interested in doing things to me which seemed to mobilize feelings in me that he wished to disown, or demoralizing me as though to fill me with depression and hopelessness. In this way he seemed to be creating a situation in which he was like an affliction, perhaps the illness his brother suffered from, while I was left like the brother (i.e. that part of himself which was identified with the brother and projected into me) in a state in which I had to struggle hard to remain analytically alive.

A Tuesday session

As usual recently John presses the buzzer continuously, and the noise reverberates throughout the whole house. As I open the door he is looking up triumphantly at his au pair, who has brought him, and she is laughing but in an embarrassed way. He says to her "Oh, sorry, I forgot" but quite insincerely. I remove his hand from the buzzer gently but firmly and say "Hello John." At the door of the playroom he asked if I would please wait outside as he has a surprise for me. I agree, somewhat reluctantly. I hear a noise that could possibly be striking matches and I open the door. He is not striking matches and although I cannot see what he is doing I wait before entering the room. When I do go in after about a minute he has arranged some sheets of drawing paper on the floor and there is obviously something under them. He treads on the pieces of paper and then shows me that he has "secretly" placed some peanut shells all over the floor under the sheets of paper. He says nothing to my enquiry as to what the purpose of this is, although I assume he intended me to walk over the paper and make the mess myself as I walked into the room.

I am now sitting in my chair and he picks up his own small chair and spins it round fast and then throws it at me with an excited expression on his face. I catch it.

Analyst: "I think you want me to feel crushed now. I think I am supposed to feel a real fool for trusting you then when we probably both knew you would play a trick on me. That made you feel that you had weakened me and then you feel excited and then everything feels out of control."

John: "By the way, I am not coming tomorrow am I? Well I can't come on Saturday." [I had had to cancel the session for the next day and had arranged an extra one for the following Saturday.] "My mother says she can't manage to bring me then as she is going out. So I'm sorry about that."

I do not know whether he is telling the truth or not. He sounds sincere but the mood of the session is so against this that I suspect that this is another trick.

John then takes a piece of string and gets me to hold one end while he holds the other.

Analyst: "I think you want me to hold on to that story whether it's true or not."

John then holds the string tight and plucks a note on it, wanting me to listen, then he asks me to do the same, which I do. Then he speaks down the string, also getting me to do the same. He expresses disappointment that words don't travel down the string.

Analyst: "You are showing me that you would like to be able to be in contact with me but it seems that it can't be with words; they don't seem to get through. I think you are saying that it only seems that we are really in contact when you have an effect on me, say by tricking me and seeing how I react to that."

John gets down, takes the string and makes a loop at one end with which he tries to lasso me. Then he climbs on to a chair.

John: "It was a trick. I can come on Saturday really. This is a boat and I am looking for a firm post to hook on to so I can pull myself in."

Analyst: "I think you feel that when I take a firmer hand with you I seem stronger to you. That makes you feel more hopeful about being rescued and you can allow there to be a Saturday session."

John had used the play materials since the beginning of the session, but there was now a change of emphasis and something of a change of purpose in the way he used them. At the beginning of the session he was intent on doing something to me; to fill me with irritation at his use of the buzzer; to make me feel tricked by agreeing to trust him by waiting outside the room and have him mess up the room. When I could interpret his wish to demoralize me and by doing so show him that I was still able to feel hopeful about my work, I believe he could then recover his own more loving self and manage to engage in much more constructive play in which the setting is used to communicate and his wish to trick me lessens as, for example, he tells me that he can come on Saturday.

John hitches the toy boat up to one of the taps and pulls the chair up to the sink. Then he gets down and ties the other end to the arm of my chair. He then acts as if he is going to climb on to the string, saying that he is going to walk the tightrope. Do I think this will be possible? I don't say anything and he puts one foot on the string, which then breaks. The atmosphere then changes immediately. He starts to fill the sink up with water and then turns his back on it as it is about to over-flow. As I get up to turn off the tap he says condescendingly, "Will you turn it off please."

Analyst: "You knew the string would break under your weight. When you felt something better was happening between us, something in you that only wants to be the star hated that and wanted to break us apart."

John seems quite oblivious of what I said, reminding me of the string telephone that won't carry words. He is busy on his own and says, half to himself, "What I need is a weight . . . Ah this will do." He picks up the small padlock from his toy box and attaches it to one end of the broken string. He whirls it around his head and lets go, allowing it to fly off at random. It hits me on the shin quite hard.

John: "I'm sorry."

He seems to mean this and yet picks the padlock up and, before I can stop him, lets it fly off again. This time it hits the wall. I get up to take it from him but he dashes across the room, grabs it, and lies down with it underneath him on the couch. I decide not to grapple with him but simply to be watchful. I go back and sit down.

Analyst: "When you broke the string you lost the feeling that you want me to help you and I think you are then afraid that I'm not strong enough to stop you and the side of you that gets so excited by battering me and the room."

John looks pale and says, "I'm tired and I'm going to sleep."

I think it is clear that the moment John had broken the string he had stopped "playing". Once more his aim was to affect me, to have me take responsibility for my own and the room's protection while he looked down on me for doing that (as evidenced by the way he conde-scendingly told me to turn off the tap). I understood the whirling padlock on the string as his excitement at relinquishing any responsi-bility for his own destructiveness and his freedom to despise me for taking up that responsibility. In doing so he was not only attacking his objects but also the part of himself that could, and earlier in the session did, take some responsibility for his destructiveness and his wish to be in contact with a good object. I believe, although I did not interpret this to him, the breaking of the string suddenly reminded him of the fragility of his objects (including, of course, his brother) and of his own mental health, and led quickly to a wave of unbearable depressive anxiety from which he fled to his manic denial of concern for himself or his objects.

Analyst: "You feel tired of all this violence but you can't bear the thought of trying to find me again and I think you're afraid I also want to give up."

John lies with his thumb in his mouth for a while before looking up.

John: "Dr Anderson, I'm trying something new. Guess what it is. It begins with D and it ends with T. I've never succeeded before. Guess."

I suggest that he wants to tell me something important but cannot quite bring himself to decide to do so.

John: "Well it has an I after the D."

Analyst: "Diet?"

John: "Yes. My mum's given me some nice soup made of vegetables."

As he is telling me this he picks up the waste bin and noisily throws it across the room.

Analyst: "You are trying to tell me something important about your-self—how hard you are trying and that you have a mother who wants to help you—but I think that the idea of the two of us working together to help you seems to be less attractive than the hard exciting way of forgetting your difficulties."

While I spoke, John was humming in a tuneless, ugly way (he has a good singing voice). It seems meant to drown out my words. If I stop speaking then he stops chanting. He starts when I start and he looks triumphant and again excited at being able to do this. I wait silently for a few minutes.

Analyst: "You would like to prevent the John who does want to speak to me and who trusts me from being heard."

John: "I don't want to come here at all."

Analyst: "That's only partly true. When you do allow me to 'pull you in', like with the lasso, because you do want to be here and hope that the analysis will help you, I think that makes you feel small and think about upsetting things and so you want to get away from it."

John is calmer and lies quietly for a few minutes.

John: "How much time is there? Don't tell me . . . it's fifteen or twenty minutes, is it?"

Analyst: "There's another thirty minutes."

John: "Scheizer. That's German."

Analyst: "I think you feel quite afraid that you won't be able to keep things all right here with all that time and won't be able to stop yourself shitting on the session, especially when we have a long gap with no session tomorrow.'

John: "Huh."

He then quickly seems to go to sleep. During this time he is quite out of contact as far as I can tell. I wake him at the end of the session. He looks cross but he does say goodbye as he leaves the house.

This is a tiny extract from an analysis that went on for a number of years and, of course, like all analyses it was unique, but I think it illustrates many of the aspects of the more recent use of Melanie Klein's technique that I have been discussing. In this session there is a great deal of activity and the interactions between patient and analyst kept shifting from periods of a calmer dialogue between them and periods when the main activity of the patient was to pull the analyst into action. I saw my task at these moments as trying to understand what it was the patient intended by his activities and hoped that by processing them that the patient would feel contained and be able to move once more to a position more of owning his own mind. In such a fragile and tense atmosphere complete interpretations in the Strachey sense were not possible, and would not have been at all appropriate because they would not have taken into account what John would be capable of hearing at that time. No doubt there are many other ways that the material could have been taken but, in looking back over it, I felt that I had mainly managed to stay in an interpretive mode rather than responding with action that John had partly hoped to pull me into. I was much more preoccupied in trying to allow John to be in a state of mind that was less driven to project and more interested in thinking, and as such I was interpreting more how he functioned rather than what the content of his phantasies were. In that sense I think it could be said that I was more interested in *psychological* rather than *anatomical* part objects. There was one point in the session where I did not stick to this approach, and I think this may have been responsible for John giving up and going to sleep in the last part of the session. This was when John used the word "scheizer". My response that he was worried about "shitting" on the session could be described as more of an anatomical part-object interpretation. In fact it was a kind of laziness on my part, born from my wish not to have to carry on trying to understand and process his material, perhaps from a kind of despair that he could not resist his wish to give up coping with his own seemingly endless pull towards destructiveness. In fact, had I managed to carry on thinking, I would have remembered that John had a German au pair who often brought him and whom he was shortly to lose. He was very fond of her and she was very good at managing him. Although, of course, he was showing off his ability to swear in German, I think he was also in a more hidden way appealing to her to help him sustain his "diet of nourishing food" rather than giving in to his wish to abandon all caution and give in to his impulses. In that sense she represented a version of me that he felt could help him carry on the struggle. An interpretation that addressed this hope not to "shit" would, I think, have been more useful. Simply being concerned with his wish to "shit" was over simple and missed the point.

All technique—and Melanie Klein's technique of child analysis is no exception—has to be understood in terms of what it is trying to achieve. Her technique was developed in terms how she understood her theories then. Thanks to her discoveries and those of her successors, our understanding about the mind has developed considerably since then and the changes in technique take account of this as they will continue to do in the light of future developments.

References

Klein, M. (1955). The psycho-analytic play technique: its history and significance. In: *New Directions in Psycho-Analysis*. London: Tavistock [reprinted in *The Writings of Melanie Klein Volume III* (pp. 122–140), London: Hogarth, 1975].

Klein, M. (1975a). *The Psycho-Analysis of Children, Volume I, The Writings of Melanie Klein*. London: Hogarth.

Klein, M. (1975b). *The Narrative of a Child Analysis, Volume IV, The Writings of Melanie Klein*. London: Hogarth.

Spillius, E. B. (1983). Some developments from the work of Melanie Klein. *International Journal of Psycho-analysis*, 64: 321–332.

Spillius, E. B. (1988). Introduction to Part One: Developments in technique. In: E. B. Spillius (Ed.), *Melanie Klein Today, Volume 2: Mainly Practice* (pp. 5–16). London: Routledge.

CHAPTER TWO

Child analysis: when?

A. H. Brafman

T he world at large interprets the word "psychoanalysis" as a reference to a specific therapy for emotional problems, but we have always stressed that psychoanalysis is also a research technique and a theory of psychology. When we mention "child analysis", however, our "public" audience again considers only the therapeutic technique, though privately we consider it important for two other reasons: (1) the light it may throw on our theories of emotional development, and (2) the role it plays in the training of a psychoanalyst. Each of these reasons deserves attention in its own right

Training

In June 1970, the European Psycho-Analytical Federation organized a symposium on "The Role of Child Analysis in the Formation of the Psycho-analyst" in Geneva; the papers given by Diatkine, Anna Freud, and Segal were published in 1972 in the *International Journal of Psycho-Analysis*: they are well worth re-reading. Diatkine focused on the treatment of children by analysis and discussed many of the problems encountered in clinical practice. His is not an easy style, but the text is clearly based on wide experience. Diatkine's description covers the multiple types of intervention that the analyst displays during his work with a child. I was particularly interested in his argument that, by interpreting, the analyst becomes a helpful figure for the child to introject. Diatkine seldom used the word transference, but he stressed how "from the very beginning of the cure the psychoanalyst should be for the child the source of both pleasure and aggression and that this ambivalence should not cease to develop thereafter." This is quite a different picture from the usual one of the "neutral" analyst or the image of the analyst who is no more than the transference construct created by the projections of the child, the "container" object.

Discussing the role of the parents, Diatkine puts forward some interesting comments. "Everyone agrees that a psychotherapeutic approach of the parents is necessary, except, of course, when one treats exclusively the children of psychoanalysts themselves, whose own analysis should suffice" (Diatkine, 1972, p. 149). And if does not suffice? This can be a serious clinical problem. But he stresses that the real parents

> must not be confused with the child's parental imagos. They can play a most important restorative or traumatic role, but they are not the original "objects" of the child, for the elaboration of object relations begins very early. The effect of therapy must be to give them the possibility of a better restorative action; it must not aim at the utopian goal of making them conform to an image of ideal parents. [ibid.]

Another illuminating comment made by Diatkine is worth quoting:

> If the parents' mental functioning has a structuring effect upon the psyche of the child, one must not forget that the child in turn structures his parents and that this essential aspect of reciprocity should not be neglected. [ibid., p. 150]

As I understand him, Diatkine is discussing analysis as therapy. He appears to take developmental theory for granted, and his frequent comparisons between the analyses of children and adults focus on the similarities and differences in terms of theory and technique, rather than on the issues taken up by Anna Freud and Hannah Segal.

Anna Freud gave a forceful paper that, strangely perhaps, still seems very topical. She described the reasons that led her to develop the training in child analysis as the primary function of the Hampstead Clinic. Anna Freud saw the child as a live field of research and she believed that the child analyst had a unique opportunity to observe how the child utilized his inborn potential to adapt to pressures from the external world. Speaking of the various ventures that became known as the "widening scope of psychoanalysis", Anna Freud argued that, of all of them, "child analysis proved unique in one all-important respect: it was the only innovation which opened up the possibility to check up on the correctness of reconstructions in adult analysis" (Freud, A., 1972, p. 153). And yet, "analysts of adults remained more or less aloof from child analysis, almost as if it were an inferior type of professional occupation". After listing the reasons usually given to justify why five times per week analysis is not feasible with children, Anna Freud commented: "It was difficult not to suspect that most analysts vastly preferred the childhood images which emerged from their interpretations to the real children in whom they remained uninterested" (*ibid.*, p. 153).

She found, perhaps predictably, that training students who had not analysed adults before,

> with only their own personal analysis as a model of procedure for adults, had, if anything, less than the average analyst's difficulty to accept a technique in which free association is non-existent; in which transference is shared with the parents; in which there is a minimum of insight on the patient's part, coupled with a maximum of resistance; where the patient's treatment alliance is unstable and precarious and needs parental assistance in times of stress; where action takes the place of verbalization and where the analyst's attention cannot be concentrated on the patient exclusively but needs to be extended to his environment. [Freud, A., 1972, p. 154]

Anna Freud wanted an institute where each trainee would have a comprehensive training, seeing adults, children, and adolescents. In practice, this entailed our British Psychoanalytical Society accepting the training of what is now the Anna Freud Centre as a valid qualification for child analysts to embark on the training in adult analysis. This conflict is still not fully resolved, but it is worth underlining the point that Anna Freud saw the analysis of children and of adults as of equal importance in the training of a psychoanalyst. Segal thought this was a deserving ideal, but she pointed out that this was unlikely ever to be achieved. She presented clinical material demonstrating how helpful it was to have experience with both a child and an adult, but she concentrated on a more limited goal.

> In our institute in Great Britain we had for years lectures on child analysis and clinical seminars, which were compulsory for all students. Unfortunately, we are going through one of our periodic great upheavals and reorganization, and I find to my horror that the child has been thrown out with the bath water: the course of child analysis for the ordinary candidate has disappeared, I hope only very temporarily. [Segal, 1972, p. 160]

She lists, therefore, her

> minimal requirements: first, full integration of theory of psychoanalytic knowledge derived from the analysis of children in teaching; secondly, baby and child observation; and thirdly, attendances at lectures and clinical seminars on child analysis irrespective of whether the candidate is treating children himself.

She adds her hope that exposure to these experiences might encourage candidates to see a child case in analysis. Sadly, the distance between the ideals of some experienced teachers and reality is far too wide, and to this day Segal's comment that many people might find her "minimal requirements already far too ambitious" still remains a true reflection of prevailing attitudes.

I have quoted rather extensively from these papers because it is important to reflect on what, more than thirty years later, has changed. "The child in the adult", "the baby part of the adult", and other such expressions have become fashionable. Those who have had children or adolescents in analysis continue to put forward arguments to convince other analysts that they should experience first hand the analysis of a child. Although I am sure that not a single analyst would say a negative word about child analysis, the vast majority of analysts nevertheless feel more comfortable working with adults. I completely share Anna Freud's view that analysts prefer to work with the "reconstructed child", that conceptual organism that we postulate underlies an adult's pathology. I was quite surprised when I first discovered students observing babies and trainees analysing children who told me that these children represented the nearest they had ever come to a child. I now know that this is far more common than I would ever have guessed.

If we are aiming at *training*, at better equipping a future analyst of adults, I subscribe to Segal's "minimum requirements", but I would add a totally different suggestion. When I started my analytic training, because my medical course had not included any long-term placement in psychiatry, I had to spend a whole year working part-time in a mental hospital. So, why not demand something similar from those candidates with no experience of children? "Infant observation" sounds a reasonable option, but, in practice, candidates are far too exposed to the preconceived theoretical ideas of seminar leaders. In terms of discovering how children think, feel, behave, and speak, it might be much more effective for candidates to spend a number of sessions at a nursery and/or infant school—not supervised or monitored, and with no reports to present, but simply observing at close quarters children living and playing together. I am sure our candidates would have a great deal to learn from the children and the class teachers.

I believe we will continue, like Anna Freud and Segal over thirty years ago, to preach that "child analysis is good for you". At any rate, we should find children and adolescents for any analysts of adults willing to analyse them. Nevertheless, I am not convinced that analysing a child is the only way of persuading analysts that our developmental theories are soundly based or the ideal way of making them familiar with the psyche of a real child. Neither do I believe that analysing a child is such an additional benefit for the work with adult patients.

Research

From Freud onwards we have made sense of adult psychopathology through our theory that links it to early infantile development.

Both instinct and object-relations theories postulate phases that the child goes through to achieve adulthood. Normal and abnormal functioning are related to conflicts and failures that can, supposedly, be resolved by our psychoanalytic techniques. In the paper quoted earlier, Anna Freud described the aims of therapy of the child very succinctly:

> [as with adults] to include the undoing of repressions, regressions and inadequate conflict solutions; to increase the sphere of ego control; and, added to this, as an aim exclusive to child analysis: to free developmental forces from inhibitions and restrictions and enable them once more to play their part in the child's further growth. [Freud, A., 1972, p. 154]

It follows from our basic hypotheses that the observation of infants and the analysis of children should give us the opportunity of putting our views to the test. In practice, we find that observations, descriptions, and interpretations are determined by the worker's theoretical framework. This can be clearly seen in reports on infant observation, where the student appears concerned, above all, with learning the teacher's preferred mode of interpretation of the findings. Considering child analysis, perhaps we should turn to Anna Freud again:

> Transference itself as a concept has changed its nature from a manifestation spontaneously arising in the patient's consciousness and behaviour to one purposefully introduced into the situation by the analyst's interpretation. [*ibid.*, p. 152]

I believe this is a perfect example of how one and the same clinical datum can be interpreted in fundamentally different ways depending on the analyst's theoretical bias.

One needs to do little more than read clinical accounts of child analysis or child psychotherapy cases: my impression is that, whatever the pathology of the child, the same mechanisms and concepts so familiar from adult analysis are resorted to in order to explain the behaviour and/or utterances of the child. Perhaps I am missing some important point, but I would like to find an account where the analyst wrote that interpretation "x" might explain the content of the child's material, but it would *not* explain why this was expressed in that particular manner. This might be the lead to take us to non-dynamic factors that I believe are very relevant to an understanding of some of the children seen in the consulting room. Perhaps I could quote from Schacht's paper published in *Psychoanalysis in Europe* (1992), in which she described the analysis of a four-year-old boy, Julian. Because Julian made frequent and vicious attacks on children at his nursery, transfer to a school for handicapped children was considered. Similar destructive behaviour occurred at home and his mother also reported that he compulsively dug, with his hands, deep holes in the garden. After he repeated this action at the analyst's house, Schacht linked this behaviour to his unconscious fantasies about his mother's body and also to the demolition of a barn where he used to play. Julian also attacked the analyst: "without warning tore my hair, tried to throw things in my face and once even scratched my eyes in such a dangerous way that I became deeply frightened and angry" (*ibid.*, p. 68). Schacht quoted many examples of Julian's compulsive repetition of words and actions. For example: "Julian kept asking me in a monotone 'what's that?', 'what's that called?' and so on— endlessly. With unusual patience I gave him answers and explanations" (*ibid.*, p. 65). Later, she wrote: "As an aside he told me that there had been a bird's nest at home and he had destroyed it. Babies had been growing in it, tiny babies. He had squashed them all. He burst out laughing" (*ibid.*, p. 75).

Schacht's moving account of an extremely difficult analysis focuses on the discussion of a particular parameter (seeing the child in another room during a limited period of regression) that proved very useful. Most interpretations centred on Julian's conflicts with his younger sibling and their mother and how these have affected his developing sense of self. Progress was noted, though there was also (on page 69) a reference to continued violence at home.

The material I have quoted reminds me of similar children I have seen. Some of them had therapy and I was profoundly disturbed when, many years later, I saw them turning up as adult psychiatric patients. Searching back for features that might have alerted me to more serious pathology I had obviously missed, I found, for example, repetitive behaviours (echolalia, perseveration, rituals, tics, games and constructions pursued endlessly, etc.), concrete thinking (learning by rote, not grasping symbolic meanings in ordinary interactions, reacting to drawings and toys as animate beings), incapacity to empathize with objects (treating people as things, lack of awareness of how the other feels) and an odd balance between affects and overt behaviour (manic reactions, panic attacks, frozen/ detached appearance: if one can consider uncontrollable anxiety as an explanation, the *degree* of the reaction still begs an explanation).

I believe that some of these features can be seen in the description of Julian and, if it is true that at times Schacht's interpretations did appear to bring relief and change in his behaviour, I find myself wondering whether this boy's difficulties can be remedied through his analysis. I am sure that he gained immensely from the help Schacht gave him, but it would be most interesting to learn how he progressed into adolescence. My suspicion is that even when relief can follow insight or some interaction that proves helpful, these children may still have some inherent tendency, weakness, or incapacity that persists throughout their lives.

I would like to quote some material from a child I observed in a group of children with developmental problems.

Joe was three-and-a-half years old when referred because of his odd behaviour, toilet training difficulties, and language delay. It gradually became clear that he presented an autistic-like picture and later on the diagnosis of Asperger's syndrome was chosen, so as to take into account his obviously high intelligence level and competence in certain areas. One day he came into the room making gentle, sinuous movements with his hands. Someone commented that this movement had been named by Joe the previous week as "the spider". Joe smiled and stopped the movement. But his mother explained that the same movements can at other times be incorporated into other games he happens to be playing. For example, they could become a flying aeroplane. The following week, Joe again made the movements with his hands, but he now gave them names: they had become Thunderbird one and two.

Joe's mother told us of an occasion when Joe complained about a hissing noise produced by a bus; she explained that this was produced by the brakes. But soon another bus came and it had a huge advert on its side, depicting a snake: Joe pointed to it, said "snake" and added the hissing noise. She thought this was funny, but she became quite perturbed when he now pointed to each bus that went by and made the same hissing noise, each time saying "the snake" and, of course, refused to climb into any of them. The difficulties of caring for children like Joe can be seen from an example where, when it was time to leave our weekly meeting, Joe lay down on the floor and raised his arms. Mother said, "No, I won't carry you, you are too heavy", explaining this often happens in shops or streets. I said that perhaps Joe wanted some comfort and suggested holding him a bit on her lap: she gave it a try and only seconds later he was willing to walk out normally.

Six months later, Joe had a new ritualized movement: he lifted his shoulders and shook his head. His mother linked this to the time when he had eczema and she had checked his back a few times. Joe greeted me warmly, as ever, and asked me for the time, a request he repeated only a few minutes later. His mother commented that this happened quite often, but added that Joe had no concept of what the answers he got might actually mean. A further six months later, Joe's vocabulary had increased, and his manner of approaching adults and children was absolutely normal as far as accepted manners are concerned. His play could appear normal even if he always played on his own (he might accept other children playing alongside him, but he never actually played with them), but every so often he would come up with a non-sequitur utterance that made us wonder about his grasp of the words he could absorb. His mother found it remarkable that he could, out of the blue, come up with a sentence he had heard months earlier when watching television. And yet, in spite of all these indications of Joe's difficulties in relating to those around him, one day he made some drawings on the blackboard. First, he called them diplodocus and tyrannosaurus rex. Then he made another huge, prehistoric looking figure with a baby figure next to it: he called them Joe and mother. Then he began to draw a father, that was obviously too big and would drown the other two, so he stopped and told me to wipe it all off. Then he repeated the same drawings, but now they were father and his sister and Joe proceeded to draw himself and mother at the other end of the board. Good, solid, orthodox, oedipal material.

Joe was placed in a small class for children with special needs and, four years later, he is starting to attend ordinary classes. He seems to do well in mathematics and can read well, but a new teacher commented that "talking to Joe is like having an echo chamber, he repeats what I say", and his contact with the children appears formal and stilted. He still cannot engage in mutual play and occasionally experiences anxiety he cannot control.

I could give many more examples of this bewildering mixture of words and behaviours that do contain meaning and others that do not appear to have it. There is no doubt that Joe can learn, but it can be difficult to assess whether he can grasp the rationale behind each new piece of learning. So, we speak of stereotypes, ritualistic behaviour, concrete thinking, incapacity to symbolize, and many other descriptive concepts, but my point is that when we have children like Joe in analysis it is not enough to interpret the content of their communications. We should also try to explore whether there is, in fact, any logic that determines whether or not they can grasp the meaning of each new piece of learning. Having observed Joe and other children like him, I am left with the impression that they can acquire new knowledge and build on some skills, but each one seems to have a number of impediments that appear not to respond to educational or therapeutic input. Surely, these are the children who would make child analysis a most valuable *research* instrument.

Our dilemma is that once wedded to the theory of developmental stages, we have locked ourselves into the straightjacket of believing that obstacles, impediments, shortcomings, failures, inhibitions, etc., can all be removed by "effective" therapy. Personally, I do not believe that we are all born with the same endowment and the same potential for development. Analysis of children gives us a golden opportunity to gain some idea of the difference between what we could term an "emotionally determined" symptom and a manifestation of some intrinsic fault in the child's mental/psychological/emotional make-up. The fact is that such an organic fault is definitely *not* a contra-indication for analysis, but we should use this analysis precisely to sharpen our understanding of the interplay between endowment and learning. Interpreting the content of the child's material can be useful, but we must keep an open mind with respect to other aspects of the child's communications if we are to take advantage of the analysis as a research enterprise.

Therapy

The European Psychoanalytical Federation has held several meetings to discuss child and adolescent analysis. In 1991, Campbell read a paper on the frequency of sessions (1992) giving very helpful guidelines to the problem of diagnosis and choice of treatment.

Campbell surveyed the literature, he quoted the results of a questionnaire that our psychoanalytic society sent to qualified analysts, and he also interviewed senior child analysts in the society. I would like to quote from this paper (p. 106) the link made by Ross (Bernstein, 1957) at the American Psychoanalytical Association annual meeting in 1957, between Anna Freud's diagnostic categories and the treatment modalities she recommended:

1. Conflicts between the child's primitive wishes and their frustration by environmental forces could be treated by counselling or therapy of the parents to correct over-severity or excessive leniency.
2. Conflicts between the child's primitive wishes and the parents would become internalized conflicts after identification with the parents and include the compulsive, over-aggressive, delinquent and over-conforming child. After the age of 6 or 7 years, once- or twice-weekly treatment was considered to be insufficient to modify the super-ego.
3. The presence of truly internal conflicts between male and female identifications, activity and passivity, and love and hate, indicate the need for analysis.

The two key concepts underlying this formulation are (a) that symptoms result from conflict between instinctual impulses and a restricting influence that comes from the environment or, later, from the super-ego, and (b) that the level of intervention is dictated by the assessment of the child's internal world. It follows from this that, when the child is very young, the parents are counselled or treated "to correct over-severity or excessive leniency", but as the child develops further and internalizes the conflicts with the parents, it is the child who becomes the focus of treatment. But what about the parents?

Campbell wrote that "it is often difficult to recommend *what the child needs* [my italics] because of the parents' motivation and pathology". This view is probably what led the discussants in the 1957 American panel to accept "that therapy was advisable for parents when their child underwent psychotherapy or psychoanalysis", much as Diatkine said more than ten years later.

I believe Campbell reflects the predominant view on child and adolescent analysis in our Society when he goes on to write that "when the recommended five-times-weekly frequency is unmanageable by the parents it is still worth working with a child on a once-weekly basis if the parents can support this." I want to discuss two aspects of this statement: (a) the treatment of the child and (b) the role of the parents.

We seem to have developed in our psychoanalytic world something akin to what is found, for example, in medicine. Some surgeons are known to be interventionists and others are considered conservative in their approach. This means that the treatment eventually offered to the patient is virtually predictable when one knows whom one is consulting. Of course, this also works the other way round, when the patient is determined to obtain a particular treatment and consults several sources until he finds someone who will recommend the treatment he wants. In the field of child analysis, it is well known that many analysts wanted their children to have analysis because they believed this would ensure their normal psychological development. This attitude duplicates the determination of other parents who will only allow their children to have once-weekly sessions. On our side of the question, we know that some colleagues argue that children should have "good analysis", that is, five or, at least, four sessions per week, while others are convinced that this is unnecessary and that children can benefit from less frequent sessions.

What concerns me is how rare a true assessment of "what the child needs" has become. Virtually all analysts and therapists see children for a diagnostic evaluation, but so often this becomes the beginning of the kind of therapy practised by that professional. In my experience, it is very rare to hear that the child was best served by a therapy that required the services of another professional. But I suspect this cannot be changed: it seems to be a manifestation, in our world, of the curious blend of knowledge and faith that affects all human beings. In other words, deciding "what the child needs" comes to depend on highly personal views and, at best, we can only aim to discuss this as much as possible among ourselves.

Turning to the parents: what do we want to evaluate? Our family therapy colleagues found a way out of considering alternatives by claiming that both the parents and the child are involved and all need treatment together. When we decide to take the child into treatment we may well recommend that one or both parents have therapy for themselves, but in practice we try to ensure that the child's treatment is not jeopardized. I would like to look at the parents' role in a different way: considering that they have helped the child to develop normally in so many other areas of his life, why is it that they now cannot help the child with his presenting problems? One answer might be that this results from the child having internalized parental figures that can no longer be affected by the real parents, but how do we establish that the parents can cope with a child who overcomes these conflicts? If a parent is unable to shift his perception of the child, can we really count on his cooperation with our treatment? Conversely, if the parent or parents are able to treat the child differently, to what extent can we involve them in the child's treatment?

I want to make it very clear that I believe that when *training* is considered, we search for a child whose parents are prepared to cooperate with the required number of attendances. "What the child needs" is still respected, but I think we are entitled to take into account the trainee's needs as well. But when there is no question of training involved and we have to decide which treatment to recommend, I feel that our diagnostic evaluation should also establish how much we can count on the parents for help. Not only "will they support treatment?", but "would they be able to benefit from knowing in what way their own conflicts are involved in the child's problems?"

Reading Stern's (1995) *The Motherhood Constellation* on his work with what is now called parent–infant psychotherapy, I found him reassuring readers that this new therapy is not a new "blame the mother" campaign (p. 21). This seemed a neat summary of an issue I had picked up when trying to justify my brief interventions with children and parents (Brafman, 1997, 2001). If we can establish the reason why the parents are treating the child in a manner that perpetuates the child's problems and we help the parents to understand the child's feelings, this can be beneficial to all of them. This is not "blaming the parents" but seeing them as a source of help for the child.

Because we have developed a theory of the psychopathology of the individual, we have come to consider, implicitly or explicitly, that therapy of the individual is the only area to which we can devote our therapeutic efforts. Of course, many will argue that one-to-one therapy is what we have been trained in. This is fair enough except when we discuss "what the child needs". Then, we must differentiate between *treating* and *conducting an assessment*.

I have quoted Diatkine on the mutual influences that child and parents exert on each other and this is a point of view now adopted by many other workers. But he did not pursue this argument to its logical conclusion. It is in the literature on parent-infant psychotherapy that we find this approach put into practice. Fraiberg (1980), Ornstein (1984) and now Daws (1989), Hopkins (1992) and Stern (1995), have demonstrated how, given the right help, parents can influence the development of their infants in a positive way. This is achieved when the parents can *change the way in which they treat the child*. I have been able to obtain similar results with older children and adolescents (Brafman, 1997, 2001), even when the symptoms seemed quite serious.

I am not arguing that we have better and quicker ways of helping children than giving them analysis. I rather want to emphasize the importance of a careful and detailed evaluation of the patient brought to us. Only then will we know precisely "what the child needs" and how we can provide for this.

In the worst possible scenario, we have parents who bring the child to us and have no capacity or wish to change their way of seeing the child. We may well decide that, even in these circumstances, we must do what we can to give the child a positive emotional experience. But when we find parents who are able and willing to become involved in the child's treatment, we should consider whether the child should be seen on his own and the parents by another therapist, or whether we should see them together, so that they can learn about each other and develop different ways of relating. Quite often, joint meetings are a valuable step to ensure a subsequent individual analysis that makes sense to the child and the parents.

Whether we like or not, there is no doubt that a full analysis is an onerous commitment for any family. Furthermore, not many children or adolescents are able to accept attending for sessions four or five times each week. I believe we do ourselves a disfavour if we are seen to recommend analysis to a child or adolescent for no other reason than that child and parents are willing to accept it. I feel that at the end of the day we should make sure that full analysis is given only to those children whose needs cannot be met by other therapeutic interventions.

References

Bernstein, I. (1957). Panel: Indications and goals of child analysis as compared with child psychotherapy. *Journal of the American Psychoanalytic Association*, 5(1): 158–163.

Brafman, A. H. (1997). Winnicott's *Therapeutic Consultations* revisited. *International Journal of Psycho-Analysis*, 78: 773–787.

Brafman, A. H. (2001). *Untying the Knot—Working with Children and Parents*. London and New York: Karnac.

Campbell, D. (1992). Introducing a discussion of frequency in child and adolescent analysis. *Psychoanalysis in Europe*, 38, Spring: 105–113.

Daws, D. (1989). *Through the Night: Helping Parents and Sleeping Infants*. London: Free Association Books.

Diatkine, R. (1972). Preliminary remarks on the present state of psychoanalysis of children. *International Journal of Psycho-Analysis.*, 53: 141–150.

Fraiberg, S. (1980). *Clinical Studies in Infant Mental Health*. London: Tavistock.

Freud, A. (1972). Child analysis as a sub-speciality of psychoanalysis. *International Journal of Psycho-Analysis*, 53: 151–156.

Hopkins, J. (1992). Infant–parent psychotherapy. *Journal of Child Psychotherapy*, 18: 5–18.

Ornstein, A. (1984). The function of play in the process of child psychotherapy: a contemporary perspective. *Ann. Psychoanal.*, 12/13: 349–366

Schacht, L. (1992). The elasticity of the setting. *Psychoanalysis in Europe*, 38, Spring: 63–80.

Segal, H. (1972). The role of child analysis in the general psychoanalytical training. *International Journal of Psycho-Analysis*, 53: 157–161.

Stern, D. (1995). *The Motherhood Constellation*. New York: Basic Books.

CHAPTER THREE

Anna Freud—child analyst*

Rose Edgcumbe

A nna Freud's contribution to child psychoanalysis is enormous. On this topic alone her publications span over fifty
years and fill several volumes of her collected works. Her
originality and clarity of thought are immediately obvious from
these written works which are, in my view, essential equipment in
the repertoire of any analyst. She also provided unrivalled oppor-
tunities for training and research in child psychoanalysis and child
development in the Hampstead Course and Clinic that she and
Kate Friedlander founded in 1952. Her influence has stimulated a
great deal of study and research, not only by workers in psychoanalysis but in several other disciplines as well.

In this short paper I can give only my personal selection of
certain important aspects of her work, which is better known in
America and some other European countries than in Great Britain
or even, surprisingly, in this Society. Indeed, it seems to have been
almost as an afterthought that her contribution to child analysis

---

*A slightly shorter version of this paper (originally entitled "The contribu-
tions of Anna Freud to child analysis") was read at a Commemorative Meeting
of the British Psychoanalytical Society on 18 May 1983.

was added when the rest of the programme for the Commenorative Meeting of the Society had already been planned, even though one stream of the Institute's training in Child Analysis is now delegated to Hampstead. The contrast between Anna Freud's international reputation, which brought her many academic and political honours, and her partial isolation in this country might, perhaps, be seen as the aftermath of the disagreements between the Kleinian group and the Viennese group of analysts, whose arrival in London in 1938 brought to a head the theoretical and personal disputes previously conducted at a safe distance.

I have no personal knowledge of those times. I first met Anna Freud in 1959 when I became a student at the Hampstead Clinic. But I think we probably have to take into account the personality of this formidable woman. Her wish for personal privacy (she refused to write an autobiography, and wanted no personal memorial at this Society's meeting) could make her seem distant and aloof; and the concise clarity of her formulations, whether in print or in spontaneous discussion, were evidence of her powerful intellect: sometimes, therefore, she was mistaken for a cool intellectual. It was certainly difficult for most of us to know her well. But as student and colleague working closely with her at Hampstead, one could not avoid experiencing the warmth of her feelings on two subjects dear to her heart: psychoanalysis, and the welfare of children. She was passionate and uncompromising both in defence of what she regarded as true psychoanalysis, and in the promotion of any aspect of child care with which she became concerned. It was this passion that stimulated all who encountered her professionally. Sometimes what she stimulated was admiration and emulation, sometimes it was disagreement. She did not always tolerate either opposition or fools gladly and could state with crushing precision her objections either to one's theoretical stance or to one's ineptitude in caring for a child. But she could also withdraw into disapproving silence, leaving the object of her displeasure uncertain of exactly how they had sinned.

The Hampstead Clinic is sometimes spoken of as Anna Freud's extended family, and that is how it often felt, with all the ambivalence such a statement implies. Large, lively, close-knit families, especially when headed by a brilliant matriarch, confer upon their members many developmental advantages and some disadvantages. They can be in turn stimulating and supportive, rivalrous and envious, cooperative or competitive, harmonious or argumentative, possessive or liberating, limiting or expanding, neglectful or caring. They attract many good friends and curious visitors who contribute to the general atmosphere of learning and enquiry. Whatever the difficulties, such families never create indifference or boredom; family members and guests alike emerge enriched, eager to develop the ideas whose seeds were sown there.

Much of what I find most valuable in Anna Freud's work centres around the development of the child growing up in the family. She thought it essential to look at all aspects of development in great detail in order to acquire a proper understanding of the needs and capabilities of the growing child. Her best known original contributions lie in the area of ego functioning. In particular, her 1936 volume, *The Ego and the Mechanisms of Defence*, remains a standard textbook. From her further work on the ways different strands of development interact, she was able to formulate a detailed psychoanalytic view of normal development as a background against which to assess the relative normality or pathology of a child according to age. Her work over several decades culminated in her 1965 book, *Normality and Pathology in Childhood*; but she continued to expand and elaborate her thinking in many subsequent papers. It was her understanding of developmental issues that shaped her views on transference in child analysis, and on the timing of the development of object relationships and internalized structures with which Melanie Klein's views were particularly at variance. It was also this detailed understanding of the child's developmental needs and capacities that made her so valuable to the paediatricians who attended her seminars for years; to the Yale lawyers she worked with on problems of legal disposal of children; to all concerned with the education and the daily care of children; and to those dealing with handicapped children. The assistance Anna Freud gave to members of other professions was of a kind that greatly enhanced the reputation of psychoanalysis. But there is insufficient space here to discuss these many applications of her psychoanalytic thinking, already published in a number of books and papers. Instead, I will concentrate on those areas most closely related to child psychoanalysis.

When Sigmund Freud first investigated the vicissitudes of instinctual development his interest focused on what was repressed in instinctual life. In the 1920s he turned his attention to the repressing forces, and thus to a study of ego functioning and development. It was in this area that Anna Freud made major theoretical contributions. Sigmund Freud defined an instinct as "a measure of the demand made upon the mind for work in consequence of its connection with the body" (Freud, 1915c). In a paper on aggression Anna Freud elaborated this:

> It is the claim of the instinctive urges on the mind which results in the development of new functions, the so-called ego functions. The main task of the ego functions is seen in the attempt to reconcile the demand for gratification made by the instinctive urges with the conditions existing in the child's environment. [Freud, A., 1949, p. 37]

In 1936 she had already discussed the view that:

> the term psychoanalysis should be reserved for ... the study of repressed instinctual impulses, affects and phantasies ... It should confine its investigations exclusively to infantile phantasies carried on into adult life, imaginary gratifications and the punishments apprehended in retribution for these. [Freud, A., 1936, pp. 3–4]

And she disagreed with this view on the grounds that:

> From the beginning, analysis, as a therapeutic method, was concerned with the ego and its aberrations: the investigation of the id and of its mode of operation was always only a means to an end. And the end was invariably the same: the correction of these abnormalities and the restoration of the ego to its integrity. [ibid., p. 4]

She went on to discuss the role of ego resistance, and its implications for transference interpretation. She pointed out that not only instinctual impulses but also ego defences may be transferred on to the analyst, and for full understanding both require interpretation.

> If we succeed in retracing the path followed by the instinct in its various transformations, the gain is twofold. The transference-phenomenon which we have interpreted falls into two parts, both of which have their origin in the past: a libidinal or aggressive element, which belongs to the id, and a defence-mechanism, which we must attribute to the ego—in the most instructive cases to the

ego of the same infantile period in which the id-impulse first arose. Not only do we fill in a gap in the patient's memory of his instinctual life . . . but we acquire information which completes and fills in the gap in the history of his ego-development or, to put it another way, the history of the transformations through which his instincts have passed. [*ibid.*, p. 21]

She went on to consider all the defence mechanisms discovered by Sigmund Freud in the analysis of adults, and added some more of her own, e.g. denial in fantasy, denial in word and act, restriction of the ego, and identification with the aggressor. She lucidly discussed the importance of distinguishing between the sources of dangers that set defence processes in train: the inner sources, instincts and affects; and external sources, unwelcome or frightening pieces of reality. She also stressed the distinction between three motives for defence: super-ego-anxiety (fear of one's own conscience), objective anxiety (realistic fear of the object's reactions), and instinctual anxiety (dread of the strength of one's own instincts).

It was in *The Ego and the Mechanisms of Defence* (1936) that Anna Freud began to work out a developmental sequence of defences, distinguishing those that require only a primitive psychic apparatus from those that depend on the attainment of more sophisticated levels of ego functioning. She developed the concept of age-appropriate defence: what is normal in childhood may be psychotic in adults. Sigmund Freud (1926d) had said in "Inhibitions, symptoms and anxiety":

It may well be that before its sharp cleavage into an ego and an id, and before the formation of a superego, the mental apparatus makes use of different methods of defence from those which it employs after it has attained these stages of organization' [Freud, 1926, p. 164]

Anna Freud expanded this formulation:

Repression consists in the withholding or expulsion of an idea from the conscious ego. It is meaningless to speak of repression where the ego is still merged with the id. Similarly we might suppose that projection and introjection were methods which depended on the differentiation of the ego from the outside world. The expulsion of ideas or affects from the ego and their relegation to the outside world would be a relief to the ego, only when it had learned to distinguish itself from that world. Or again, introjection from the outside world into the ego could not be said to have the effect of enriching the latter unless there was already a clear differentiation between that which belonged to the one and that which belonged to the other . . . Sublimation, i.e. the displacement of the instinctual aim in conformity with higher social values, presupposes the acceptance or at least the knowledge of such values, that is to say, presupposes the existence of the super-ego. Accordingly, the defence-mechanisms of repression and sublimation could not be employed until relatively late in the process of development, while the position in time which we shall assign to projection and introjection depends upon the theoretical standpoint which happens to be adopted . . . According to the theory of the English School of analysis, introjection and projection . . . are the very processes by which the structure of the ego is developed and but for which differentiation would never have taken place. These differences of opinion bring home to us the fact that the chronology of psychic processes is still one of the most obscure fields of analytical theory. We have a good illustration of this in the disputed question of when the individual super-ego is actually formed. [1936, pp. 55–57]

She hazarded a guess that:

Such processes as regression, reversal, or turning round upon the self are probably independent of the stage which the psychic structure has reached and as old as the instincts themselves, or at least as old as the conflict between instinctual impulses and any hindrance which they may encounter on their way to gratification. We should not be surprised to find that these are the very earliest defence-mechanisms employed by the ego. [*ibid.*, p. 56]

The book contains a number of illuminating discussions of examples of defence sequence in the analysis of children from which I have space to select only one: her re-examination of Sigmund Freud's account of Little Hans (Freud, 1909b) who, you will remember, had a fear of being bitten by a horse. Anna Freud says: "Here we have a clinical example of simultaneous defensive processes directed respectively inwards and outwards" (Freud, A.,

1936, p. 75). She describes how aggressive oedipal impulses towards his father

> roused his castration-anxiety—which he experienced as objective anxiety—and so the various mechanisms of defence against the instincts were set in motion. The methods employed by his neurosis were displacement—from the father to the anxiety-animal—and reversal of his own threat to his father, that is to say, its transformation into anxiety lest he himself should be threatened by his father. Finally, to complete the distortion of the real picture, there was regression to the oral level: the idea of being bitten. The mechanisms employed fulfilled perfectly their purpose of warding off the instinctual impulses; the prohibited libidinal love of his mother and the dangerous aggressiveness towards his father vanished from consciousness. His castration-anxiety in relation to his father was bound in the symptom of fear of horses, but, in accordance with the mechanisms of phobia, anxiety-attacks were avoided by means of a neurotic inhibition—Little Hans gave up going out of doors. [ibid., p. 76]

> Even after analytical interpretation had enabled Little Hans' instinctual life to resume a normal course ... he was constantly confronted with two objective facts with which he still could not reconcile himself. His own body (in particular his penis) was, of course, smaller than that of his father ... Thus there remained an objective reason for envy and jealousy. Moreover these affects extended to his mother and sister ... because, when his mother was attending to the baby's physical needs, the two shared a pleasure, while he himself played the part of a mere onlooker ... At the end of his analysis Hans related two day-dreams: the phantasy of having a number of children whom he looked after and cleansed in the water-closet and, directly afterwards, the phantasy of the plumber who took away Hans' buttocks and penis with a pair of pincers, so as to give him larger and finer ones. [ibid., pp. 76–77]

> The phantasies helped him to reconcile himself to reality, just as his neurosis had enabled him to come to terms with his instinctual impulses ... Hans denied reality by means of his phantasy. [ibid., p. 78]

> This mechanism belongs to a normal phase in the development of the infantile ego, but, if it recurs in later life, it indicates an advanced stage of psychic disease. [ibid., p. 85]

The examination of developmental issues was pursued in many papers after 1936 as Anna Freud gathered data not only from her own patients but from the many child analyses carried out at the Hampstead Clinic, as well as from observational data gathered in the Well Baby Clinic, the Nursery School, the Nursery School for Blind Children, the Mother and Toddler Group, and the earlier War Nurseries.

Much of this work is distilled in the "Developmental Profile" and the "Developmental Lines", and is brought together in her 1965 book *Normality and Pathology in Childhood*. The Profile, or, to give it its full title, "The Metapsychological Profile of the Child", began in a research group on diagnosis, with Anna Freud setting down on paper the framework of theoretical understanding and clinical experience that she had in the back of her own mind when assessing a child. It started as an attempt to help diagnosticians refine their psychoanalytic assessment of a child's psychopathology and treatment needs by ensuring that due attention is given to all relevant aspects of a child's prevailing psychological status, developmental history, and family background. Its aim is to keep a balanced perspective, to prevent one's thinking from being skewed by a symptom seen in isolation, by one outstanding feature of the family, or by some passing fashion in diagnostic categorization. Above all, it aimed at keeping in mind what would be age and phase appropriate for a particular child with a particular combination of constitution and life experience. Instead of diagnostic labels, it arrives at a psychoanalytic statement as to whether the child's difficulties reflect a transitory disturbance normal for the child's developmental phase, or explicable as a reaction to external stress, or whether the difficulties are a sign of more permanent fixation and regression due to internalized conflict or another serious deviation from normal development, taking into account which areas of psychic functioning are disturbed. Such terms as neurotic, psychotic, or borderline are only very rough approximations to the more detailed assessment required to predict what an individual child needs in order to get back on to the path of normal development.

Originally intended for diagnostic assessment of children, the Profile has subsequently been used to assess treatment results and for research and teaching purposes. It has been adapted for use with other groups, such as adults, adolescents, babies, and handicapped children. It has been modified in many ways, sometimes expanded, sometimes shortened and simplified. Those who are not familiar with it sometimes find it too obsessional or time-consuming, because they mistakenly regard it as a detailed questionnaire to be laboriously filled in. Properly used it need not even be written down, being simply a theoretical framework for organizing one's thoughts about a patient's material in the light of one's relevant clinical experience. All good diagnosticians have some such framework, and the Profile is Anna Freud's.

The Metapsychological Profile was soon supplemented by the Developmental Lines. These are deceptively simple formulations of stages of development in a number of areas of a child's everyday behaviour, showing what aspects of psychological development and functioning underline the achievement of successive stages on each Line. In addition to diagnostic purposes, they can also be used to assess a child's readiness for, or likely reactions to, such ordinary life experiences as entry to nursery school, separation from parents, birth of a sibling, hospitalization, etc. The Lines first delineated by Anna Freud in 1965 were:

- From Dependency to Emotional Self-Reliance and Adult Object Relationships.
- From Suckling to Rational Eating.
- From Wetting and Soiling to Bladder and Bowel Control.
- From Irresponsibility to Responsibility in Body Management.
- From Egocentricity to Companionship.
- From the Body to the Toy and from Play to Work.

She and others have since added further lines.

I called the Lines "deceptively simple" because although the descriptions of each stage are brief and make use of observable behaviour, it takes a psychoanalyst to get the most out of such observations and to understand the full import for differential diagnosis and distinguishing between stages. For example, on the Line from Suckling to Rational Eating, throughout the first four phases food is equated with mother. Food refusal and food fads therefore indicate difficulties in the mother–child relationship, and so can sometimes be circumvented by another person feeding the child. Following traumatic separation in these early phases, food refusal indicates rejection of the mother-substitute, greed and over-eating mean treating food as a substitute for mother-love. In phase five, however, the equation food equals mother fades out and irrational attitudes to eating are determined by sexual theories and fantasies. Eating disturbances are now no longer related to the external object, but are caused by internal structural conflicts, and so are not affected by the material presence or absence of the mother.

It was such detailed awareness of children's development that shaped Anna Freud's views on child psychoanalysis. She says, for example:

> It is to be expected that, owing to their immaturity, children lack many of the qualities and attitudes which, in adults, are held to be indispensable for carrying out an analysis: that they have no insight into their abnormalities; that accordingly they do not develop the same wish to get well and the same type of treatment alliance; that, habitually, their ego sides with their resistances; that they do not decide on their own to begin, to continue, or to complete treatment; that their relationship to the analyst is not exclusive, but includes the parents who have to substitute for or supplement the child's ego and superego in several respects. Any history of child analysis is more or less synonymous with the history of efforts to overcome and counteract these difficulties. [Freud, A., 1965, pp. 28–29]

She points out that:

> The adult's tendency to repeat, which is important for creating transference, is complicated in the child by his hunger for new experiences and new objects. Assimilation and integration, which are essential helps in the phase of "working through", are counteracted in the child by the age-adequate emphasis on opposite mechanisms such as denial, projection, isolation, splitting of the ego. [ibid., p. 27]

She continues that the urge to obtain gratification is much stronger in children than adults, which creates difficulties in the analysis. But against this:

> the urge to complete development is immeasurably stronger in the immature, than it can ever be in later life . . . the child's unfinished

personality is in a fluid state . . . Libido and aggression are in constant motion and more ready than in adults to flow into the new channels which are opened up by analytic therapy. [*ibid.*, 1965, p. 28]

On questions of technique Anna Freud particularly stressed that even children who can communicate verbally do not free associate, and that play and action are not completely satisfactory substitutes, even if only because it is often impossible to tell whether the child is communicating about a piece of external reality it has experienced, or a fantasy from its own inner world. In the 1920s, when child analysis was in its early experimental stages, Anna Freud thought that the child's dependence on its parents and age-appropriate caution with strangers would result in mistrust of the analyst that could only be overcome by an introductory period during which the analyst made friends with the child, gaining its trust and confidence, and encouraging a positive transference (1926). She subsequently abandoned this view, when it became apparent that analysis of defence could allay the child's initial anxieties (1945). One of Anna Freud's outstanding differences of opinion with Melanie Klein concerned transference; and although Anna Freud altered her views over the years, there remained a wide gulf. She said, for example, in 1965;

I have modified my former opinion that transference in childhood is restricted to single "transference reactions" and does not develop to the complete status of a "transference neurosis". Nevertheless, I am still unconvinced that what is called transference neurosis with children equals the adult variety in every respect. The question whether this is the case or not is all the more difficult to answer since it is obscured by two of the peculiarities of child analysis . . . without the use of free association not all the evidence for the child's transference appears in the material; and owing to the child's acting instead of associating, the aggressive transference is overemphasized and overshadows the libidinal one. [Freud, A., 1965, p. 36]

The main reason for Anna Freud's doubt that children can develop a full transference is the child's real, age-appropriate and normal dependence on his real, external parents, which is quite different from the adult's internal dependence on fantasy parents, and which makes the child incapable of becoming wholly involved with the analyst in a way which contains the neurosis in the transference. Her stress on the child's real involvement with and dependence on his parents does not lead her to believe

> that alterations in external reality can work cures, except perhaps in earliest infancy . . . Every psychoanalytic investigation shows that pathogenic factors are operative on both sides, and once they are intertwined, pathology becomes ingrained in the structure of the personality and is removed only by therapeutic measures which effect the structure. [*ibid.*, p. 51]

In the late 1960s and 1970s Anna Freud turned her interest to the psychoanalytic categorization of childhood symptomatology and to the problems of technique in working with emotionally deprived and socially disadvantaged children, and those with non-neurotic disturbances such as various forms of developmental delay and deviation (Freud, A., 1970, 1972, 1974, 1979). She thought that an analytic technique based mainly on the interpretation of conflict is inappropriate for such children, since their disturbances are often not due to conflict in neurotic form but are more in the nature of personality stunting or deformation acquired in the process of adapting to an inadequate or malign environment. But she strongly believed that one should try to help such children, and that such help required even more intensive individual work than child analysis. A good deal of such work goes on at Hampstead. My own experience is that usually what starts out as something modestly called "developmental help" eventually turns into something more like analysis proper, as the child improves enough to develop an organized neurosis. For example, in the treatment of a four-year-old girl who was disorganized, passive, under stimulated, under-functioning, dissatisfied, and miserable, and came from a large, impoverished, and disorganized family with a depressed mother, the turning point came when she could formulate the following question to her therapist: "How do I be proud of myself?" This question provoked much discussion in a study group on technique, raising issues of handling narcissism, object relations, identification, self-esteem, and so on. Anna Freud summarized her own ideas on how best to approach this child's problem in her suggested answer: "That's a very difficult question, but I think that when I am proud of you and when you like me, you will certainly be proud of your-self" (Freud, A., 1983, p. 115).

This kind of simplicity in interpreting to children was charac-teristic of Anna Freud. She did not go in for long, complicated inter-pretations, but rather made them sound like ordinary conversion. To take another example, this time of a common neurotic fantasy: a child

> imagines his mother is a witch and this comes into the transference, where he would be afraid of the analyst, the witch. One would not immediately interpret the past, one would react by saying, "Me, a witch? It must be somebody else", which is a transference interpret-ation. [*ibid.*, 1983, p. 122]

Anna Freud's capacity for simplification, which sometimes seemed like over-simplification, made any meeting or seminar a memorable experience. One usually came away feeling first enlight-ened, and then provoked to further questioning, which is, I think what she wanted. I would like to close with another excerpt from the transcripts of the discussions on technique:

> What we are working for in child analysis is a model technique; and after all, all our students join us in the experiment to find that model technique. Every single supervision hour is experimental in the sense that we continue to try, again and again. What else can we do? [*ibid.*, 1983, p. 120]

References

Freud, A. (1926)[1946]. Introduction to the techniques of the analysis of children. In: *The Psychoanalytical Treatment of Children* (pp. 3–52). London: Imago.

Freud, A. (1936). *The Ego and the Mechanisms of Defence.* London: Hogarth Press.

Freud, A. (1945)[1946]. Indications for child analysis. In: *The Psycho-Analytical Treatment of Children* (pp. 67–93). London: Imago.

Freud, A. (1949). Aggression in relation to emotional development: normal and pathological. *Psychoanalytic Study of the Child, 3/4*: 37–42.

Freud, A. (1965). *Normality and Pathology in Childhood*. New York: International Universities Press.

Freud, A. (1970)[1972]. The symptomatology of childhood. A preliminary attempt at classification. In: *The Writings of Anna Freud, Volume 7* (pp. 157–188). New York: International Universities Press.

Freud, A. (1972)[1982]. The widening scope of psychoanalytic child psychology, normal and abnormal. In: *The Writings of Anna Freud, Volume 8* (pp. 8–33). New York: International University Press.

Freud, A. (1974)[1982]. A psychoanalytic view of developmental psychopathology. In: *The Writings of Anna Freud, Volume 8* (pp. 57–74). New York: International Universities Press.

Freud, A. (1979)[1982]. Mental health and illness in terms of internal harmony and disharmony. In: *The Writings of Anna Freud, Volume 8* (pp. 110–118). New York: International University Press.

Freud, A. (1983). Seminars on technique. *Bulletin of the Hampstead Clinic*, 6: 1.

Freud, S. (1909b). Analysis of a phobia in a five-year-old boy. *S.E.*, *10*: 3–149.

Freud, S. (1915fc. Instincts and their vicissitudes. *S.E.*, *14*: 109–140.

Freud, S. (1926d). Inhibitions, symptoms and anxiety. *S.E.*, *20*: 77–175.

CHAPTER FOUR

Being Frankenstein: a youth's solution to psychosis

Edna O'Shaughnessy

I am looking back at an analysis which took place nearly forty years ago. A twelve-year-old boy came to me, mentally broken down. After three years of analysis he left, at his urgent insistence, able to resume his life and his education, while maintaining a projective identification with Frankenstein.

I present this paper as a case study which raises a number of questions. What was the nature of my patient's recovery? What was the role of the analysis in this recovery? How can we try to understand his bizarre identification with Frankenstein?

Case study

Hugh's parents told me his history. He was their youngest child, born when his mother was under great stress coping with a house that was too large. At just six weeks of age, the housekeeper thought Hugh screamed because he needed a bottle to supplement breast feeding. But despite being given a bottle, Hugh continued to scream. Later, Hugh disliked school and did little and poor work at a succession of different schools. His education stopped finally when his father brought him home, weeping and panic-stricken, from a weekly boarding school. From then on Hugh was at home, unable to be alone, unable to go out, or let his parents go out together. He ruled the household. His parents told me about what they called his "habits", Hugh's chief one being the collecting and storing of rubbish. They also told me that an elder son had been born with a physical disability, and that they were desperate for Hugh to have a good education. They were angry with Hugh (especially his mother), and frightened, as well as concerned and worried that they demanded too much of him.

When his father brought Hugh to the first session, I saw a beautiful, sad boy with a nice smile, rigidly clutching his father. In the playroom Hugh was terrified, and clung to a small chair. He gazed out of the window to empty his mind or looked, not at me or the furniture, but at the spaces between. From his fearful hovering gaze I could tell that these spaces seemed to him to be full of particles. At moments he seemed curious about the open drawer full of playthings, but self-contemptuous and expecting contempt from me if he showed any interest. Unspontaneously—he needed the prompt of a question from me—he spoke a few words, while rubbing finger and thumb together. I spoke to him about all the things he had allowed me to observe on this first day.

On the second day, Hugh brought two books and a newspaper with him. On the cover of *More about Paddington* was a picture of a small bear on a cushion, which I understood as his picture of himself, a small bear like Paddington, in a new analysis that was a cushion for him, and that he wanted to tell me more. Hugh stared anxiously at the wall, minutely rubbing his belt, eventually telling me he was watching a hand pointing a finger. He moved the book aside to reveal headlines on the newspaper: "BOY FRIEND, EXTRA". I interpreted that he felt frightened and pointed at, accused of masturbation, and he wanted me to know that his penis was like something "extra", a boy friend to hold on to in a frightening world. Hugh felt himself to be in a space of small particles and over-sized looming things, another of which was a watching eye on the latch of the window. The little chair he held on to, like his penis, or his father, or myself, signified real objects that stopped him from succumbing to psychotic panic in this menacing space of fragments and bizarre objects (Bion, 1957).

While terrified and placatory, from the start of the analysis Hugh was also grateful and gained relief from having his terror and the nature of his threatening world recognized. He often murmured an affirmatory

"Mmmm". He communicated through morsels of sometimes confused speech, body movements, pictures, and headlines in newspapers. Once he was able to sit down, he played a little with toys and paper. Mostly he made vivid drawings for which he had a gift.

He began to carry a transparent bag containing a book called *A Creepy World* with him everywhere he went. I understood this as his ideograph (Money-Kyrle, 1965) for his belief that, like the book inside the bag, he was with his creepy world inside the analysis. Some days he lost his capacity to distinguish the real world from his psychotic world, which was always there. Then, with finger movements, or the flicker of an eye muscle, or the grinding of a top tooth on a bottom tooth, he launched attacks on enemies in order to survive. Pulverizing persecutors made him fear a return attack from small things; any slight noise or movement made him rigid with fear. He drew bits, pieces, and vague trailing shapes, and I came to know what he already knew, that he felt in danger of bits from his self and his objects seeping out in his breath and speech or his hands as he drew, and getting confused with me and the room. To staunch and to recoup his losses he had to be sparing of movement and words, take his drawings home, and whenever he saw a piece of fluff or speck of dirt he put it in his pocket. "One of my habits", he told me tonelessly.

In a needed omnipotent phantasy, Hugh felt me as continuously with and around him until I told him about the Easter break. He swung round and stared at me, his face wide with the shock of disbelief. The next day he came bearing a drawing of misaligned concentric circles with a sunken gap. He said accusingly, "England and France were once joined. Then a volcano came and they got separated. The middle bit got sunk and now they are like this", pointing to the mismatch, the sunken bit and the gap. I said he was showing me what I had done to him. He no longer felt as he had before that, whether we were near or far, we were linked and I was around him. My words about the impending holiday had pushed into him and made him sink in the middle. Hugh drew a moon with four rockets round it (he had had four sessions so far), which he said dropped darts of air on to the moon and then there would be enough air to live. He farted again and again, frantic when he could not stop. He drew an earth and a distant moon with craters, which the four rockets were leaving. In sum, Hugh responded to the first separation with elemental intensity, a characteristic of psychotic children described by many authors, including Winnicott (1945), Mahler (1961), and Tustin (1972, 1986). The shock of my withdrawal left Hugh sunk and angry, his orifices open and incontinent; he accused me of failing to match his unlimited need of me to always be round him and to breathe life into him. He was left like a dead moon, marked by the craters of my and his violence.

After this first break Hugh's beauty vanished. He returned with sores and pimples round his mouth, a cut on his thumb, dirty, and dim looking, like a too-long-neglected infant. With trembling hands he took from his drawer a paint box he had not touched before. He withdrew it from its wrappings and grew calm as he gazed at the colours. I spoke to him about his feeling in the holiday that he and I were dead and how seeing the colours meant there was still life here. But life had changed.

Instead of his *Creepy World* book in the transparent bag, Hugh brought a flicker booklet. By flicking its pages he made a "film" of a figure jumping up from the end of a seesaw so that the figure on the other end was shot into space and the two figures changed places in the air and landed on the opposite end of the seesaw. Hugh often anxiously halted the film with a figure stranded in the air to picture his chronic anxiety that at any moment I could get up and go, and hurtle him into space. He could, and did, reverse our places and make me know and endure his position by keeping me stranded in horrific silence for long hours. Hugh brought a cloth cap with a press-stud on its "flap" and pressed the press-stud in and out, to show me his repeated attempts to push back objects that kept pushing him out in order to escape his flap, i.e. his anxiety. Rosenfeld (1965) emphasizes that this is central to psychotic object relations. In this battling, hostile world, also very characteristic of his parents, who were trying to get him out and moving, Hugh showed me his subtle methods of entry and control. He made paper squirrels and frogs with extending tails and tongues, and drew eyes on stalks. Specific omnipotent phantasies emerged about how the flatus from his tail, or his spittle, or his tongue, indeed any organ or body product, could dart out to bridge the gap between himself and an object, enter it, and control it. In consequence, his world was threatening and eerie: invisible threads and wires connected him to objects.

He also brought two boomerangs, which he threw repeatedly towards the wall, saying despondently, "They never go anywhere, they just come back to me", which I understood as his showing me how his signals were not received. He conveyed intense despair, still feeling himself to be a neglected baby, not a youth, whose parents (as I could observe for myself) did not comprehend the enormity of his mental handicap, distress, and anxiety. He represented them by circles containing swastikas, and as devils with horns. Hugh was excited by, and admiring of, his "opposite of the ordinary" ways, as he called them, his omnipotent masturbation phantasies (such as his secret methods of entry and control) that, for him, were concretely realized. Indeed, his contemptuous refusal at home even to try "ordinary" ways was one of the many sources of his parents' resentment.

With analysis, Hugh's bizarre world and psychotic anxieties receded. He perceived again, in his own fashion, the ordinary world and took from it the minimum necessary for survival by a process I thought of as accretion. For example, when he saw me he squeezed the muscles round one eye so that it flickered like a camera eye and "took" me. In this way he accumulated picture slices. I think all his senses were impaired and had become mechanical collectors of sights, noises, words, etc., acquiring not vital introjects but concrete bits and pieces.

At home he became able to remain alone, at first for brief periods. Then he made expeditions on his own to his local town. In my notes of that time, I recorded that he was much less anxious and more alive. Hugh started lessons again with a private tutor. His parents were enormously relieved. They soon insisted, in my view prematurely, that he make the journey to his sessions by country bus, train, and London underground, alone. Except for one or two days when they yielded to his entreaties to be brought by car, Hugh came on his own, sometimes suffering horrendous levels of fear, which his parents, recognizing that he needed to be pushed out and persecuted by their bondage to him, could not allow themselves to know.

Hugh had been in analysis for a year when he made a declaration, "I can now see two-way traffic; last term in the road there was only one-way traffic. But now there are some road-works at the top of the hill." This represented his acknowledgement of a two-way interchange of work between him and me. That evening his mother telephoned to complain that she was unbearably depressed, Hugh was impossible, and she could not stand it. The next day Hugh cancelled his appreciation of the day before, saying, "Why do I have to come? I don't find you do anything", after which he collapsed into worrying about "bits of dirt shining in the sun", the rubble of our two-way work. Here was a first glimpse of how recognition of helpful object relations precipitated an unbearable depression which he at once projected, after which he destroyed both the self and the object that were helpfully linked (cf. Segal's account of depression in the schizophrenic (1957).

Nevertheless, a new era had begun. Over the next months, though short-lived, there were sequences of acknowledged two-way endeavours between Hugh and myself, the most intense occurring when his parents went away for two weeks on their first holiday in years. Alone, Hugh made the long journeys to and from his sessions. He felt his parents had been torn out of him, leaving a hole from which more and more of him was lost each day. He stood at the window watching leaves being blown by the wind and told me in a voice choked with fear that there was a tree without any leaves on it. This was his ultimate dread: he would fall to pieces, be dispersed like leaves in the wind and cease to exist. By the end of the fortnight he had come to a virtual standstill.

Hugh's crisis in his parents' absence repeated his traumatized reaction to the first analytic break, but with a difference: he now had an object to come to. Afterwards he was movingly grateful. During the following weeks our relations were more alive, and full of contradictions. Hugh felt needy, grateful, resentful of his dependence, and hated all these feelings. He made a puppet of paper and string, explaining that the strings went into the puppet and held its bits together and that the strings pulled the puppet along and made it walk. The puppet expressed the truth of his invaded and controlled world of omnipotent psychotic phantasy, but, as a model, it completely negated the human side of our link.

In the next analytic break Hugh's experiences again contained more human elements. On the Monday of his return he spoke of a Morse code buzzer with a missing part, of its needing to be picked up, of his wanting to send messages, and of its being recharged when the two parts were fitted back together. But by the end of the week Hugh had turned sullen. He saw me as "Snow White", who turned him into one of her inferior dwarves. He had brought with him "a green man tied by strings to a parachute" and he dropped the green man repeatedly on to the table so that it pulled the parachute down. Concentrated and thoughtful, he said, "The green man is too big for the parachute." On the Friday, Hugh came for the first time with his Frankenstein mask, and a newspaper.

He placed the papier-mâché mask on the newspaper saying, "It's a mask I made of Frankenstein. It's Frankenstein's monster, but I call it Frankenstein." He made a speech. "Frankenstein is human, not a robot. There"—and he indicated the wound with stitches he had drawn on the mask's forehead—"he got hit with a chair when he went mad and broke the wires that held him. There should be a bolt"—he meant the bolt in the monster's neck—"but I did not put it in." He rubbed the back of the mask where there was an opening, saying, "I cut it down the back." Then he moved the mask aside to reveal an advertisement in the newspaper: "LONDON PRIDE—BEAUTY IN BLOUSES", after which he completely ignored me and gave all his attention to Frankenstein. I said he had turned away from me, whom he saw today as full of pride, as tying him to the analysis like a bottle puppet, so that he missed it in the holidays and wanted it like a breast, the beauty in blouses. I said he wanted me to understand he had human feelings: like the green man he felt too big to be tied to me. Later Hugh said, "The monster is grey-green, hard and not soft, and the professor made him from old things dug up from graves." I spoke about how he was losing his new, worrying mixed feelings about me by breaking his ties, and digging up old things, and being like Frankenstein. As the session neared its close Hugh grew dead-looking. I said that hardening and escaping from being what he called "a bottle puppet" deadened his feeling of being alive and there being colour in the world.

From then on Hugh always brought the mask with him. He remodelled it, sat with his head in it, or related Frankenstein's story over and over again as if it were his own. Hugh knew the story not from Mary Shelley's book *Frankenstein, or The Modern Prometheus* (1818) but from Wale's 1931 film in which Boris Karloff plays the monster. In the film, Frankenstein the scientist transgresses the limits of nature and makes a living creature, a monster that he then rejects. This story had great appeal for Hugh. It expressed his deep sense of rejection by his objects and his painful feeling of being different from others. Because Frankenstein is monstrous only through rejection and being misunderstood, it freed him from the anxiety and depression of being "a green man", whose narcissism and envy pull his objects down. Hugh claimed an affinity with each element of the tale. He would tell me how Frankenstein was not born but built bigger than normal by science from old things dug up from graves, pointing out that he had made his papier-mâché monster from bits of old newspaper and glue. He was describing a Promethean act of self-creation, a transmuting of dead bits and pieces into a being whose birth and care was not owed to parents and whose current better state was not owed to analysis. He often restitched the wound on the mask "where Frankenstein got hit with a chair" to close the wounds of separation through which he himself felt he disintegrated. By making an ever-present artefact, which he could get into and out of, one that was a victim of rejection and maltreatment, Hugh, in his omnipotent phantasies, freed himself from dependence on, confusion with, and fear, guilt, and envy of, his ambiguous objects.

Hugh put his Frankenstein mask in a suitcase and carried it with him everywhere. He made a drawing of "a framed picture of Frankenstein".

Frankenstein occupied the entire picture. Outside the frame was a small podgy face, about which Hugh said contemptuously, "It is ordinary, it has a low forehead, it is not intelligent." He continued, "The monster has a high brow and is intelligent, and there is more of him." This mental state, in which Hugh projected himself into and identified with Frankenstein was never, except fleetingly, undone in the analysis.

For reasons of space I omit the details of the period in which I struggled with a patient who was mostly almost unavailable. Sometimes Hugh played or acted being Frankenstein, sometimes Frankenstein was a mask behind and in which he could hide; often Hugh felt changed, that he actually was Frankenstein. There were cycles when his contempt for me and his excitement escalated and he grew alarmingly mad and manic, followed after a while by a collapse when, with pain and despair, he would say something like, "Shadows are real" and be, in his way, more in contact for a few sessions. Nevertheless, Hugh did not wish to relinquish his Frankenstein; his aim, it emerged, was to learn how to avoid madness, mania, or despair and he secretly listened to what I said for this purpose.

Though his "habits" (such as collecting bits of rubbish, which for Hugh was the retrieval of lost fragments of self and objects) continued, there was ongoing improvement both at home and at school. In analysis Hugh became more split, and projected on to me all opposition to his Frankenstein state of mind. He brought a gadget with a skinny hand that shot out to snatch away money and maintained this was what I was: a robber stealing money from his parents and, more immediately, aiming to steal his Frankenstein from him. For the first time since the start of treatment Hugh began to nag his parents to stop. He found them willing allies. Enthusiastic about his improvement (he was now attending a crammer and coping with larger groups of children and several teachers), they felt everyone's energy should be directed at placing him in a good school.

Very occasionally Hugh's lost self returned in horror. He would say, "Frankenstein is not real", or "Frankenstein is a kind of dead thing." Even if relieved for a while, despair, anxiety and suspicion of me drove him back to idealizing Frankenstein who brought him another sort of relief by shedding anxiety and despair, gaining a feeling that all his problems were solved, plus excitement and energy at his triumph over me with his "opposite of the ordinary" solution by means of the monster. The end of his analysis was approaching. Hugh said one day that he had been thrown in his judo class and had hurt his foot. He then talked about an old television cartoon, *Top Cat*, where an alley cat saw an abandoned baby in a park. I said he saw the ending of the analysis as his parents and myself abandoning a baby. He said he was tired and had been working at his history last night. He rubbed his fingers backwards and forwards saying, "Crooked, not straight", and spoke about vampires, werewolves, and then, with an arch intonation, Poe's *Tales of Mystery and Imagination*. I thought he was pointing out that while he had his stories, the grown-ups had Poe, which he thought had a rude meaning, so the grown-ups too had their unreal, lavatory phantasies and were not really straight. I said he was in despair about his analysis stopping. It seemed to prove I was crooked: how else could I abandon him?

Hugh could feel despair for only a moment. To his last session he brought two books and laid them on the table. One was his judo book, which had a picture of the judo expert pulling his opponent down on the cover. The other was called *Frankenstein's Revenge*. These were the powerfully controlling images through which we were both meant to view the ending of Hugh's analysis.

I was left feeling low, anxious about my patient and anxious about my work.

I had two later communications from Hugh: a letter telling me he had passed his school exams, and a few years after that, a coloured postcard of a peacock fanning its tail, on which Hugh wrote to say he had finished his course of study and obtained his diploma.

Discussion

Hugh's identification with Frankenstein, as an outcome of a psychoanalysis, is perturbing. Yet, he started his analysis broken down and when he left, he could function. How can we make sense of this?

As I see it, because I recognized that he was broken down and struggling with psychotic panics in a bizarre universe that was his mental world outside of him, Hugh could expose more of his condition to me and feel it was known. And because I spoke in an analytic way, he felt I was not submerged by his psychosis and so he could hold on to me, even though, as we have seen, his experience was that we were linked in intrusive and abnormal ways. Even so, our "two way traffic", the analytic work, enabled Hugh to recover.

This recovery put him in a predicament that he saw as "too big", i.e. beyond the limits of himself and his objects to resolve. You will recall Hugh's recognition of being helped, of neediness, of feeling more alive when with the analyst—as well as dwarfed and humiliated, believing the analyst to be full of pride, purifying herself to snow-white, disavowing her own deficiencies in understanding him. In addition, although he was better, Hugh's "creepy" world, his vulnerability to disintegration on separation, and the envious "green man" in him who deadened and fragmented, were all still uncured.

Fearing breakdown again, Hugh saw it as "more intelligent" to break his ties and project himself on to a new identity, the hard impervious Frankenstein monster, a second skin in Bick's terms (1968), or an identificate as described by Sohn (1985). Monstrous, with a justifiably black and distorted vision, ingratitude and unreality, and carrying dangers of madness and mania, Frankenstein nevertheless rendered Hugh many services: he appeared to integrate Hugh's fragmented mind into a coherent identity, he was not humiliated, but bigger than normal, and he disposed of fear and guilt. Moreover, he was always there and so closed the wounds of separation through which Hugh disintegrated.

Very near the end, again using the phrase "too big", Hugh said, "The rest is too big", and a few days later he related the first and only dreams of the analysis.

> I had three dreams. In the first dream I was emptying bits from my pockets and my mother was crying. I went up to her to put my arms around her [he started laughing] and my mother turned round and said, "Don't worry, I am going to kill you." [I interrupted to remark that he was laughing only because his dream was so frightening. He said dismissively, 'It was scary in the night' and continued telling me his first dream.] 'I woke up and I must have turned round because I went to sleep with my blanket round me and my arm under it, and when I woke up'[voice was throttled by anxiety] I was round the other way and my arm was out. I got out and ran away.

I asked if he knew why he went to his mother in the dream. He answered, "Because I was sorry." I then spoke to him about his deep unhappiness, and the fact that he was sorry that his habits upset his mother and he wanted her to know he was sorry. I suggested that he was terrified of turning round and reaching towards her because, as he saw her in his dream, she would not accept his apology—the mother in his mind was murderously revengeful. There was a long pause.

Then Hugh said bleakly, "In the second dream you pursued me to my home and whichever way I ran, you caught me." I spoke to him about how he was appealing to me to understand that he felt it was impossible for him to stay in analysis or to admit being sorry about ending it because he saw me as pursuing him to rob him of the home and the protective blanket that Frankenstein represented for him.

After a pause he said, "In the third dream there was a big hunt and I was with the great hunter. I was looking at a picture where guns were hidden." This third dream represented Hugh's tragic answer to the monsters in his inner world: they were deadened into being merely pictures and he joined the hunters, his murderous super-ego and pursuing analyst, and himself became the hunter Frankenstein.

We can now see Hugh's plight and his limits more fully. His objects were monstrous, cruelly un-accepting and vengeful. Although in external reality this was to some extent true, this was by no means the complete picture; these monsters were full of his deadly projections. Hugh functioned with a preponderance of death instincts and registered few benign experiences—for example, he deadened even the small event of his analyst recognizing that he laughed out of terror when he related his dream about the murderous mother. His narcissism was at variance with his unlimited dependence, and his intolerance of frustration was at variance with reality. In omnipotent phantasies he intruded into his objects and hated and feared return invasions from anything alive. He fragmented and deadened experience (see Feldman, 2000). Hugh knew he did this and regretted it.

But working through the binding and modifying of conflicts and feelings was "too big" a task, it was beyond the limits of the ties that existed between Hugh and his objects. Indeed, any further evolution of their relations, Hugh believed, would threaten him with paranoid and/or depressive breakdown. In despair, he broke away from his objects and, like a modern Prometheus, aimed to construct an artefact and, by intrusion into it, to gain a new existence and identity. It is important to mention that near the end of the analysis, as Hugh remodelled his mask, it increasingly came to look like his mother. For Hugh the moments when he recognized he had not after all made a transcendental escape, but that his "new" identity was an old maternal monster, were moments of horror, rapidly negated.

Hugh was limited, on the one hand, by objects with whom there could be little working through and who threatened deterioration and, on the other, by the limits of his belief in his artefact. Total belief would make him mad and manic, but if he did not believe enough, he would recognize his object as a fraud, or feel that after all he had not escaped, but was imprisoned inside his old monstrous object. Hugh had to find a position between psychotic breakdown at the one extreme and madness at the other. He aimed for a mental state that maintained a projective identification with a "new" object that served as both his container and a protective hard mask, while hedging—often by means of jokiness—his knowledge of what was real and what was unreal, as deadening, fragmenting, and rejecting psychotic episodes continued, along with some live, though aberrant, mental activity. In this way Hugh was able to ward off breakdown and madness, and continue to function.

Is it right, though, to describe Hugh's psychic limits without bringing in my limits as his analyst? Is not such a one-sided approach even outrageous? My work certainly had its limitations. There are several things that I would now do differently, and I will mention just two examples here. First, there is the question of language. Especially in the initial stages, I used too much part-object body language. Hugh's parts, like his wholes, were not natural entities like the breast, penis, or person; they were bizarre bits and entities. I conflated my world and his, and Hugh did not forget or forgive this error. Remember how on the day he first brought the Frankenstein mask, he brought also the newspaper headline: "London Pride, Beauty in Blouses". I also worry that later in the analysis I allowed myself to be too strongly controlled into fitting in with his Hugh–Frankenstein world. Anxious about destabilizing him, I did not find a way of really addressing either the distortion and deadening of which this dominating vision was the concrete end result, or his attachment to me, which was also "somewhere" unavailably there. Nor did I deal adequately with its defensive services against multiple anxieties.

Colleagues will surely have other criticisms of my understanding and work with Hugh, and have suggestions of their own to make. I am not trying to argue that Hugh could not have had a different or a better analysis. However, I do contend that Hugh would have had some such limited and quasi-delusional outcome with any analyst. Freud (1911c) described such an outcome in relation to Schreber as follows, "The delusional formation which we take to be the pathological product, is in reality an attempt at recovery . . ."

Had Hugh stayed longer what might one have hoped for? Not for normal progress, with attempts at the integration of split and projected parts of the self, mourning or Oedipal resolutions (see Steiner, 1996). Psychoanalysis is not the modern Prometheus. As Bion observed, the psychotic personality does not become non-psychotic, but has its own aberrant evolution. I would have hoped that Hugh might have been able to find a less bizarre object as his identificate. I would also hope, when I think of the world of monsters which he briefly allowed to come alive in his three dreams, that more analysis would have lessened his horrific anxiety about a murderous super-ego and a pursuing analyst. However, it may not have been possible, given our problems with "two-way traffic" and Hugh's huge anxieties about any good development, for Hugh to acknowledge that I could come to know his and my limits and that I was not demanding he be other than he was, without his being precipitated into a deep, even suicidal, depression.

The questions I ask in this paper about limits are the questions I ask myself when I look back and try to understand my own disturbance and anxiety. What were Hugh's psychic limits? What were the limitations of my work then? And what were my limitations when compared with other colleagues? What would the limits be today, when there have been advances in psychoanalytic understanding and I am more experienced? What are the limits of any psychoanalysis? And finally, when I think of the urgency of his insistence that the analysis end, I ask myself whether Hugh himself knew his own limits and stopped while the going was good.

References

Bick, E. (1968). The experience of the skin in early object relations. *International Journal of Psychoanalysis, 49*: 484–486. Reprinted in *Melanie Klein Today, Volume 1* (1998). London: Routledge.

Bion, W. R. (1957). Differentiation of the psychotic from the non-psychotic personality. *International Journal of Psychoanalysis, 38*: 266–275. Also in *Second Thoughts*, 1967. London: Heinemann.

Britton, R. (1998). *Belief and Imagination*. London: Routledge.

Feldman, M. (2000). Some views on the manifestation of the death instinct in clinical work. *International Journal of Psychoanalysis, 81*: 53–66.

Freud, S. (1911c). Psycho-analytic notes upon an autobiographical account of a case of paranoia. *S.E., 12*: 9–82.

Mahler, M. (1961). On sadness and grief in infancy and childhood: loss and restoration of the symbiotic love object. *Psycho-Analytic Study of the Child, 16*: 332–351.

Money-Kyrle, R. (1965)[1978]. Success and failure in mental maturation. In: D. Meltzer (Ed.), *The Collected Papers of Roger Money-Kyrle* (pp. 397–406). Strath Tay, Perthshire: Clunie Press.

Rosenfeld, H. (1965). *Psychotic State: A Psychoanalytical Approach*. London: Hogarth.

Segal, H. (1957). Depression in the schizophrenic. *International Journal of Psychoanalysis, 37*: 339–43. Reprinted in *Melanie Klein Today, Volume 1* (1998). London: Routledge.

Shelley, M. (1818)[1969]. *Frankenstein, or The Modern Prometheus*. London: Oxford University Press.

Sohn, L. (1985). Narcissistic organisation, projective identification and the formation of the identificate. *International Journal of Psychoanalysis. 66*: 201–13. Reprinted in *Melanie Klein Today, Volume 1* (1998). London: Routledge.

Steiner, J. (1996). The aim of psychoanalysis in theory and practice. *International Journal of Psychoanalysis, 77*: 1073–1085.

Tustin, F. (1972). *Autism and Child Psychosis*. London: Hogarth.

Tustin, F. (1986). *Autistic Barriers in Neurotic Patients*. London: Karnac.

Winnicott, D. W. (1945). Primitive emotional development. *International Journal of Psychoanalysis, 26*: 137–143. Also published in *Through Paediatrics to Psychoanalysis*. London: Hogarth.

CHAPTER FIVE

How come your house never falls down?*

Luis Rodríguez de la Sierra

João's mother telephoned me in the autumn of 1998, saying that she was worried about her nine-year-old son and wondered if she could come to talk to me about him. I indicated that it would be a good idea if her husband could come along also. She told me that he was away on a business trip and she very much wanted to talk to me as soon as possible, so I gave her an appointment for two days later. She is an attractive woman in her late thirties, well dressed and slightly over made-up. There was something a bit anxious and irritating in her manner. I detected a subtle hostility in her, which provoked some negativism in me. I was bothered about my reaction to her, which I questioned. She spoke in broken, heavily accented English, and never spoke to me in her mother tongue in spite of the clear indication that I also spoke it. She is the youngest of a family of four girls and she described a rather typical, close Portuguese family background. She told me that she was quite concerned about her youngest son who, for the last few months, had

---

*A slightly shorter version of this paper was read at the English-Speaking Weekend Conference in London, on 14 October 2000.

been exhibiting a somewhat precocious and provocative sexual behaviour, i.e. talking about sex, making sexual gestures, easily stripping off his clothes, using four-letter words, etc. João was also very jealous of his thirteen-year-old brother Xavier, and kept complaining that his parents favoured him. He also said he was unhappy at home. On the other hand—she said—he was very popular at school, where both his peers and his teachers, apparently, thought highly of him. He admired his older brother enormously and got on well with him. The relationship with his father, though, was not so good. She seemed perplexed by the fact that, although he claimed not to like his father, his behaviour became worse when father was absent, like now, for instance. Xavier, on the other hand, gave them no reason to worry. I suggested we should meet again when her husband returned. She said she would try her best to persuade him to come; he travelled often and worked all the time so she did not know if he would find the time.

A week later they both came to see me: a handsome and likeable couple who immediately conveyed a certain tension between them. They had come to England eleven years ago, because of the father's occupation. They both come from an upper-middle class background. Mr Y is a short, handsome, and friendly man who dresses very smartly. He is the eldest of a family of three, with a sister two years younger and a brother in his early thirties. His father, to whom he had always been very close, had died two years previously, which had saddened him terribly. He was also concerned about João but, unlike mother, not so much about the so-called sexual precocity which, insightfully, he saw as connected to feelings of jealousy, envy, and admiration towards his older brother. He thought that was João's unconscious way of identifying with his pubertal sibling (Xavier), in an attempt to win the attention he thought his parents gave Xavier. However Mr Y's main concern was João's apparent hostility towards him. The mother interrupted at this point and reproached him for not spending enough time with his younger son and for being too disciplinarian with him when they were together. She told me he never played with João, only tried to make him do his homework, etc. The father seemed embarrassed and tried, in vain, to reason with her. As the meeting continued it was clear that mother resented her husband's frequent business trips and that she felt abandoned and unsupported in the task of dealing with her sons, João in particular. I voiced these thoughts, and although they appeared taken aback and said that they had not thought about it in this way, my observation made sense to them. I sympathized with mother, alone in a male household and deprived of the female support she would have enjoyed in her original family. I thought I could understand better, now, the hostility towards me, yet another man, which I sensed during my initial consultation with her.

The father then added that he had never seen the boy's sexually provocative behaviour and, with a smile and in Portuguese, he said: "Typical, isn't it?" ("Típico, não é?"). I did not know if the comment referred to the boy's behaviour or if that was the father's way of seeking my support/complicity by making such a comment about "nagging" women (his wife in this case) to another man. I was aware of the danger of Mrs Y feeling excluded. He also said that the boy alluded, occasionally, to dreams, but never told him anything about them. He then told me that even if it was true that they (he and his wife) had their differences, they both loved their children and wanted to do whatever was necessary for their happiness. She agreed but said—with a certain pleasure—that they often argued in front of the children because her husband undermined her in front of them. He replied immediately that he would try not to do it again, but that it was not his fault completely because she provoked him by undermining him, in his absence, with her much more lenient attitude towards João. They both added, simultaneously, that the elder son never gave them any trouble. I ended the session by saying that the best thing would be for me to see João twice and have him tested by one of the psychologists at the Anna Freud Centre. I offered to see him the following week.

João came to see me the following Monday at 5 p.m., accompanied by his father, who greeted me warmly. João initially appeared rather reserved, but followed me willingly to my consulting room. He is a very good-looking, fair-haired boy, with huge blue eyes and long eyelashes. João was immaculately dressed in a rather continental-style adult little suit that made him look like a little man, suggesting perhaps some pseudo-maturity. I noticed that the style resembled his father's.

There was an intelligent and inquisitive expression on his face. He seemed to be covering his anxiety bravely, but I sensed his tension about meeting me. I felt sorry for him and liked him at once. I smiled at him and he appeared to relax and started talking to me in Portuguese. He said they thought they were going to be late because the traffic was heavy and his father had been late to collect him; he had just arrived from a business trip abroad. I said it must be difficult to come to see me, a complete stranger whom he had never met before. He nodded silently. I asked him if he knew what I was and if he knew why he was coming to see me. He replied that his father had told him that I was a nice man, a doctor who helped naughty children. I wondered what he meant by that and he told me that he was disobedient with his mother and, at times, was also rude to her. There was a brief pause and he added that his mother nagged him all the time and was always telling him off for not doing things the way she wanted. He then broke into English: "Do you see many children?"

I invited him to tell me what he thought and then, in Portuguese, he told me that he knew I saw children because his father had said so. I asked him which language he wished to use and he replied that although his written Portuguese was "not so good", he spoke both Portuguese and English perfectly. He then added that he preferred to speak Portuguese with me. At home, he said, he spoke it with his father all the time, because his father always used that language with him. With his mother, though, he alternated between English and Portuguese because his mother sometimes spoke to him in English. I found myself wondering about the mother's behaviour. I thought about her broken English and found myself thinking of the possible unconscious reasons why she would speak to João in a language other than her own. I have always been struck by the difficulties that must exist in the parent–child relationship when the parents choose to talk to their children in a language that is not their mother tongue and that, very often, they do not speak well.

Relationships and communications are not solely and purely based on language, of course, but I have always wondered about the quality of the relationship when one of the parents is communicating with his children through an artificial, disguised, "as if" aspect of himself. I wondered if, by not talking to João in Portuguese, mother had denied her son access to a more intimate, close contact with her.

João then noticed a box on the table and looked at it with curiosity. I said there were toys, games, crayons, and other things inside. Did he perhaps want to have a look? He smiled broadly and said: "Yes, let's see what's inside!"

He selected a pack of cards and wondered what we could do with them. "We can play any game you like", I said. He paused for a moment and invited me to try and build a house with them. I would build one and he would build another one. I succeeded in building mine. He tried very carefully to build his, but it fell down on each attempt. I noticed he did not give up easily, but persevered. I asked myself what was the nature of his communication to me as expressed through the card game. What were his anxieties about himself, about his environment? He was disappointed when the session ended, asking: "May I come back another time to continue this game?" I said: "Of course, next week, same day and time."

When we returned to the waiting room, his father smiled at us and, looking at João, wondered if he had enjoyed it. João said he had. "Good!" The father had spoken in Portuguese and, in the same language, I said that his son wanted to come back next week. Mr Y replied that, unfortunately, he would not be able to bring him because he had to go abroad again and would not be back in time to collect João. His wife, though, would bring him to me. "Is that all right?" he asked João. The boy shrugged his shoulders and suddenly looked sad.

The following week, his mother brought João to see me. They were ten minutes late and Mrs Y apologized profusely: she had been delayed by a telephone call from her mother and therefore she had been late to collect João from school. He seemed quiet in contrast to his mother, who came across as fussy and rather smothering. He withdrew physically from her when he saw me. I was struck again by the artificiality of his mother's unnecessary use of English with the two of us and noticed that he also spoke to me, or rather whispered, in English. As soon as we entered the consulting room, he asked me—in Portuguese—if I had brought the cards, and invited me to play the same game we had played the previous time. Again the results were the same: his attempts to build a house of cards failed. He would not give up, though, and indeed persisted several times but, at one point, he stopped and told me that he dreamt "every night" and that his dreams, at times, were bad ones. I asked him if he would like to tell me, for instance, his dream from the previous night. He seemed taken aback and said he could not remember. He added that he often forgot his dreams but that he knew in the morning that he had dreamt. He had tried to tell his mother sometimes, but she never seemed to have time because they had to rush to school in the mornings. I said that I thought he was trying to show me some of the difficulties he had with his mother and I wondered how he felt about discussing them with a stranger. He replied that he wanted to because Xavier was always on their mother's side and their father was very busy with his work, so he had no one to talk to. He paused for a moment and then said that he liked making things with his hands and colouring "something". I did not understand what that something might be and I said so. He replied that, if I wanted, he would show me next time. I agreed. I then realized I had not spoken to him about his seeing the psychologist who was going to test him as part of the assessment process, but I knew that his parents had told him and his mother had arranged for him to go to see her this week and the following one. I reminded him of all this and said that perhaps he could return to see me on Tuesday, rather than Monday when he would be seeing the psychologist. He did not reply.

When we returned to the waiting room, Mrs Y anxiously asked: "Did he do all right?" João looked rather diminished by this and moved to the other side of the room. I thought again that there was a fraught quality to their relationship and I wondered to what extent João's withdrawal was an expression of his being either annoyed with his intrusive mother (because he might have felt exposed by her anxious question) or of his feeling embarrassed by her attitude. I also wondered about his ambivalent communication about dreams and, initially, questioned myself for not having followed my temptation to make an interpretation about what I felt might be his unconscious motivation for doing so. Was he apprehensive about divulging too much about himself if he told me the dream? Was he thus recreating the sexual teasing of his mother or trying to convey his feelings about his father's absences? I then remembered a quotation from Anna Freud: "The analyst's task is not to create, i.e., to invent anything, but to observe, to explore and to understand and to explain" (Freud, A., 1969, p. 153).

I was, nevertheless, left with an uneasy feeling about João and his mother. I sensed a certain hostility towards him in her and I wondered how much of it was displaced from the hostility that I had noticed she expressed towards her husband. I was again puzzled by my reaction to her: I found her irritating and annoying and I was unable to know if the feelings came from me or from her. I decided to follow Anna Freud's advice and wait to see what happened.

A week later, João returned. He was his usual immaculate self, now on time and with a big box in his hands. The nanny had brought him: a pleasant young Portuguese girl with a warm and broad smile. While still in the waiting room, he said the nanny had come today because his mother had already accompanied him to see my "friend", the psychologist (a woman), thus implying that his mother did not have time to bring him twice in the same week. The place was too far away, he said, as if trying to excuse his mother. João then followed me and, once inside the consulting room, he told me that he had brought the box with the objects he had mentioned last time. It was a collection of beautiful little soldiers made of wood and painted in brilliant colours.

He announced, full of pride: "I painted them. Do you like them?"

I asked him if he had any thoughts about whether I did or not but he pretended to ignore me and instead told me that a teacher at his school liked them very much and had complimented him for his good taste. Apart from expressing his wish that I like them, he seemed to have read my thoughts. I said that I thought he was telling me that being liked was important to him and that perhaps he wanted to know if I liked him as well as the little soldiers. He nodded silently and looked at me expectantly. I asked him then if he liked coming to see me. He said he did because we talked and his parents had told him that he could tell me everything. It sounded more like a question than a statement and I voiced this. He nodded again. I said that perhaps he was not sure he could tell me everything because I had noticed, the previous week, a certain reluctance on his part to tell me his dream. He paused for a moment and said: "It was just a silly dream."

But he then told me about it.

He had dreamt about a lady who had gone on a skiing holiday and she had got lost and was trying to see if she could find the others, but she could not. She then started skiing up and down the mountains and she had an accident. When the doctor arrived, he could not cure her.

He smiled and repeated that it was only a silly dream. Other dreams were frightening, but not this one. He then stood up and went to the window and tried to open it because he felt, suddenly, that the room was too hot. He could not open it and asked me to help him, which I did. He went back to his chair and looked inside the toy box. He got out some dolls: father, mother, grandfather, and two children. Then he went to the soldiers and said they were going to fight because they were at war and, for a while, he played with them. He stopped and directed his attention towards the family dolls. He said grandfather had died because he was afraid of the war. [I made a mental note about the reference to his own grandfather's death.] The daddy doll was curious about the war that was going on outside and left. The mummy doll started crying because one of the children was ill and she did not know what to do.

I said I thought he was worried about himself and also about his family and was asking me if I could really help. I also thought, but did not say to him, that he resented my sending him to see the psychologist. I wondered if he had interpreted that as a rejection or as an indication that I needed the help of others to deal with him, like his parents. I also thought that the dream possibly contained hostile wishes against his parents, particularly against his mother. I wondered, as well, about his excitement *vis-à-vis* the possibility of having found someone for himself, me. [The Portuguese word he used for "mountains", *serra*, sounds very similar to part of my surname and actually means the same.]

He asked: "Well, can you help me?"

I replied that I did not know if I could, but that the two of us might try to understand first what was wrong and then we both would be in a better position to say if I could help. I wondered if he would like to come to see me more often and he said he could come after school if his mother had time to bring him in. I said I would talk to his parents and they would tell him when he could come to see me next. If he wanted, I said, he could come to see me every day from Monday to Friday, and then we could talk a bit more about his dreams, both the "silly" ones and the "bad" ones. He replied that he would very much like to do so.

After he left, I thought again about his dream and wondered how sensitive João was to his mother's feelings of sadness about being in a foreign country, feeling lost in a male household, and being without the support of the female members of her family. I then thought I could understand more about my initial reaction to her and wondered if her reluctance to speak to me in Portuguese was her way of showing me all that: was she conveying to me that using English was her dogged way of trying to adapt to a new country as well as her way of avoiding missing her country and family, which she would do if she used her mother tongue? "*Olhos que não vêm, coraçao que não sente.*" (What the eye sees not, the heart does not rue.) I thought João's dream also told me something about his possibly conflicted female identification.

I telephoned his parents and arranged for a meeting with them. I explained that both the psychologist and I felt that João needed, and would benefit from, intensive treatment. To my surprise, they seemed relieved and agreed without much fuss. I then said that although I would want to see them once a term to discuss how things were going, I would not be able to see or speak to them more often than that. The mother immediately wondered what they would do if they felt they needed to talk to me because João could be rather difficult at times. I said that I would like them to see a colleague whom they could see once a fortnight or monthly if they so wished. They accepted and we agreed that João would start his analysis the following week.

While I have no doubts that the parental pathology influenced João, I was convinced that the boy had internalized conflicts that he dealt with through the defensive use of externalization, by making them appear as conflicts with his external world, with his objects.

João started his analysis in February 1999. The initial stages were spent mostly with a variety of games and the occasional session where he would draw, showing a promising artistic talent. From time to time he chose to talk and when he did so, there was a pseudo mature quality to his conversation. His games, though, appeared appropriate for his age.

Two or three times a week we would play the "build a house" game with the playing cards inside his box. His house would always collapse. I felt intrigued by this intelligent, charming little gentleman, inexplicably clumsy when it came to playing that game. Although he emerged as a very bright boy in the psychological testing, non-verbal skills appeared erratic. This was most noticeable while trying to build the house. Towards the end of the first term, it seemed that this was not due to any deficit but rather to conflictual interference. From time to time, he would also bring the wooden soldiers and one day (a Wednesday) I thought I was seeing some clinical indications of his aggressive impulses and wishes to retaliate. Two soldiers were fighting, one small and delicate, the other big and strong, with a moustache and a beard. The little soldier tried to start a fight with the bigger one several times, until the bigger one warned him. The little soldier persisted and then the big one kicked him. I said that perhaps he felt annoyed with me at times, for instance, when he tried to build the house and failed while mine stood up. He ignored me and continued playing. I said that perhaps he did not want me to notice these things because he was not sure yet that he could talk to me freely, without being afraid that I might be annoyed with him and retaliate for his hostile feelings towards me. The following day he was brought by the nanny, who explained that Mrs Y had guests from abroad and could not come. João reported a dream:

He was coming back home from school, at night, when a big black man tried to steal his backpack. He tried to run but he could not move; he tried to cry for help but he could not utter a word.

I thought that his aggression, and his anxiety about punishment, was expressed in the dream. It conveyed a strong sense of guilt, as well as a sense of failing "to get away with the crime". I said it sounded like a rather frightening dream. He nodded, paused for a moment, and then laughed and said: "Don't be silly, it's just a dream."

I could see, more clearly than on other occasions, how he used denial as a means of defence. He was silent for a few minutes. He then said that he wanted to bring the little soldiers again because I had liked the way he had painted them, but had forgotten to do so because he had got into trouble with his mother. He was playing with some friends and she was nearby and had got angry with him because he was telling some dirty jokes. She told him off and threatened to tell his father, who did not allow four-letter words at home. I thought João's dream could be understood along the lines of castration anxiety. His dream followed a session where his play showed fantasies of mutual aggression. The black man who steals his backpack is a condensation of both his fears of being attacked and deprived of a highly valued possession and of his own retaliatory wishes. The backpack is nothing but a disguise for his "front-pack", his genitals. He confirmed this in the session by "forgetting" to bring his precious little soldiers (which he assumes I like), a symbol of his genitals. I believe he "forgot" because he feared, unconsciously, I might steal them from him.

Just before telling me the dream, he gave me an association to a situation where he behaved in a sexually provocative and excited way (telling "dirty" jokes), which he "exposed" to his nearby mother. She reacted by threatening him with the image of a castrating father with whom, I believe, she gets confused in João's unconscious fantasies. I asked him if he had any ideas as to what this dream might be about. He moved his head silently from side to side. I said that I knew it was "only a dream", but that I also knew that dreams told us something about fears we had, and of which we were not necessarily aware. He listened attentively. I said that I thought that his dream might contain thoughts about us and asked him if it was possible that sometimes he might be afraid of me and of doing things that would make me angry. I added that he might fear what I would do to him if I got angry with him: that I might behave like the big black man in the dream or like an angry rejecting mother/father who did not like the four-letter words.

"No, you never get angry, anyway!" he replied. "My mother says you are very serious and that you have a very deep voice", he added, imitating my voice and trying to mock me. I thought that he could accept my interpretation only by his defensive use of displacement (it is the mother who fears me and not him), as well as by trying to transform passive into active (plus possible intimations of identification with the aggressor), that is, ceasing to be the one who fears me and transforming himself into the one who laughs at me.

Afterwards, I thought that the dream might also contain anxieties about having to learn another language— i.e. which language to use with me or how to speak to me. Again, I thought of the identification with his mother and wondered if the dream revealed something related to it: similar anxieties about having to learn another language and, like her, a conflict regarding how and when to use it. The homosexual content of the dream and the confusion it engendered contributed to increase João's anxiety. I also wondered if the dream, in addition, might contain the memory of a developmentally earlier anxiety dream experienced before language had partially or fully developed. A dream from pre-verbal times when he might have already experienced his mother as detached or perhaps unobtainable.

In his earliest statement about children's dreams, Freud said: "The dreams of young children are pure wish fulfilment and for that reason quite uninteresting compared with the dreams of adults" (Freud, 1900e, p. 127, n.). Both in 1905 (p. 161)[1] and in 1916 ("Introductory lectures on psycho-analysis", p. 126), he modified his views, especially in 1916: "Dream-distortion sets in very early in childhood, and dreams dreamt by children of between five and eight have been reported, which bear all the characteristics of later ones."

In 1925, however, Freud stated for the first time: "Experience has shown that distorted dreams, *which stand in need of interpretation* (my italics), are already found in children of four or five" (Freud, 1900 [1925 revised edition, p.127, fn. 1,]).

In 1927 Anna Freud said:

> When it comes to dream interpretation . . . we can apply unchanged to children what we have learnt from our work with adults. During analysis the child dreams neither less or more than the adult; and the transparency or obscurity of the dream content is, as in the case of adults, a reflection of the strength of the resistance. Children's dreams are certainly easy to interpret though in analysis they are not always so simple as the examples given in *The Interpretation of Dreams*. We find in them all those distortions of wish fulfilment that correspond to the complicated neurotic organization of the child patient. [Freud, A., 1927, p. 24]

In a previous paper, I have commented that psychoanalytic authors with very few exceptions agree that the dreams of children contribute to the insight that we can gain into children's inner worlds (Rodríguez de la Sierra, 1996, p. 72) When Freud said of children's dreams that "They raise no problems for solution" (Freud, 1900a, p. 127), it is difficult to understand how he could put forward this view that seems, by definition, incompatible with his theories about child sexuality. Paradoxically, his attitude in attributing innocence and purity to children's dreams was curiously similar to what those before him thought about children's thoughts and inner worlds. His initial formulations do not seem to take into account evil dreams, traumatic dreams, anxiety dreams, and the many nightmares that we know also occur. The dreams of children, as we can see in those of João, also possess, in addition to or "in lieu" of a wish fulfilment, a symptomatic value which should make us consider their developmental significance. They can show us the important concerns and tasks for children at different phases of development and in the course of their analyses, where they must be understood, also, in the context of the developing transference (Rodríguez de la Sierra, 1996, pp. 76–78). It was this latter aspect of João's dreams, as reported by him in the last two sessions that I have shared with you, which I chose to take up with him.

Like others, I often wonder if the interest in object relations, narcissism, attachment, transference phenomena, etc., has turned analysts away from the view, to which I subscribe, of the interpretation of dreams as "the royal road to our knowledge of the unconscious activities of the mind" (Freud, 1900a). At the same time, I no longer believe in the idea of dreams being only the fulfilment of a wish. There are dreams that refer also to fears, to reflections, and that contain memories. They can also reveal something about the developing ego of the child, particularly in relation to functions such as verbalization, language development, etc. The recognition of transference manifestations in child and adult analysis enables us to recognize the different and often complex aspects of the transference as they appear in the dreams of our patients. As we know, analytic dreams may be indicative of resistance, alliance, or both in relation to the analyst and the analytic process. The fact remains, though, that in spite of the apparent revival of interest in dreams, children's dreams continue to be neglected and thus it is not surprising that in a book as fascinating as *The Dream Discourse Today* (Flanders, 1993) there is hardly any mention of the subject of children's dreams (Rodríguez de la Sierra, 1996, p. 76).

Towards the end of his first year of analysis, João emerged as a boy who was struggling with strong Oedipal anxieties exacerbated by his father's continuous absences and by his internal representation of the father as a severe and potentially dangerous rival. Succeeding was therefore a frightening risk for him, as he showed me repeatedly by not being able to master the (phallic) game of building (erecting) a house of cards. In addition he was still engaged in a complex relationship with his mother. At times he related to her in a sado-masochistic way to which he often regressed whenever his Oedipal attempts to seduce her failed. He felt rejected by her and would try to capture her attention through his provocative, apparently precocious, pseudo-sexual behaviour. By adopting this behaviour, I thought (like his father), that he was trying to identify with his admired and envied pubertal brother, whose good relationship with his parents made him very jealous. The brother was a suitable object on to whom he could displace many of the feelings towards his father. Through the identification (with his brother), he could also keep up the homosexual attachment to both father and brother. When his attempts to deal with his Oedipal anxieties failed, João would regress to a developmentally earlier phase with overtones of his oral and his anal–sadistic struggles. His Oedipal conflicts seemed to be further complicated by the fact that it appeared (both in his play and in the transference) as if the mother was at times experienced as the castrator. Then the father became the object by whom he felt protected (as seen at the end of his first interview with me, when he looked sad and disappointed that his father was not bringing him to the following appointment).

After a year in treatment, an incident occurred which provided a turning point in the analysis: The previous summer, after many years of deliberation and even more years of depending on my old manual portable Remington typewriter, I plucked up courage and decided to buy a personal computer (a "laptop"), in the hope that it would make my life easier. I soon discovered the opposite.

This coincided with the closure of the London Clinic of Psycho-Analysis (where I had always seen all my child patients) due to the move of the Institute of Psycho-Analysis to new premises, which were not to be open for some time. I was compelled therefore to see this particular patient at my own consulting room, not far from the old Institute. I had installed both the computer and my Remington, side by side on the same desk, in my consulting room and one day, a Thursday afternoon at 4.20 p.m., it was time for my session with João. For the first time, he noticed the computer and as soon as he saw it, he was fascinated by its presence. He was delighted with the idea of the many games we could play on it, which he asked to do. He could not believe it when I said I did not know how to use the computer very well. I had sensed, immediately, his apprehension, his suspicion that I might be telling lies, that I was playing tricks. I had always been aware of his acute sensitivity to falsity in his objects.

"Really? I don't believe you; you are having me on," he said. "It's so easy that even a fool like me can do it."

João is far from being a fool, quite the opposite, but I felt humiliated in my ignorance. He seemed disappointed. And then the Remington caught his attention.

João: "What is *that*?"

His voice was full of surprise, curiosity and astonishment. A typewriter, I announced victoriously. João wanted to know what the typewriter was for, and once I explained he came to the conclusion that he would never be able to learn how to use such a mysterious and complicated machine! He spent the rest of the session trying to decipher the secrets and intricacies of the intriguing contraption. Finally, with some hesitation, he proposed an exchange. Although he still believed that I was mocking him by pretending not to be able to use the computer, he would go along with me and we would play a new game in which he would teach me how to use the computer, while I would undertake the "awesome" task of trying to teach him to use the typewriter. This, of course, was a defining moment in the analysis. The next session he brought another dream:

"I dreamt that the Pope was getting bored in Rome because he had no friends and his housekeeper kept nagging him. Fidel Castro heard about it and because they had become good friends, he invited the Pope to go to Cuba to play football with him. The Pope accepted the invitation and wanted to stay in Cuba, but the Swiss Guard did not want him to and ordered the Pope to return to Rome because Fidel was a communist and a bad man."

[The words for "Pope" and "Dad" (papa/papá) are very similar in Portuguese, as they are in other Latin languages.]

My association and counter-transference reaction to João's dream were Calderón de la Barca's words when in "La vida es sueño" ("Life is a dream") Segismundo tells us:

> Pues que la vida es tan corta,
> soñemos, alma, soñemos
> otra vez; pero ha de ser
> con atención y consejo
> de que hemos de despertar
> deste gusto al mejor tiempo
>
> [Calderón de la Barca, 1998 (1636) p. 173]

> (And since life is a dream,[2]
> let's dream, my soul,
> let's dream, my soul,
> let's dream again but this time with attention
> and bearing in mind that at some fine time
> we're going to wake up from this pleasure.)

I found out that, the previous weekend, a friend of the family had brought a video recording of the Pope's visit to Cuba. Before telling me his dream, João had said that his mother had told him off for being naughty because he had eaten his brother's dessert. After telling me his dream and ignoring both computer and typewriter, he suggested that we should play, once again, his favourite game with the cards: to build a house. We played at least five times and for the first time, he said: "How come your house never falls down?"

"Because I am not afraid that mine will," I replied. He looked at me inquisitively. I said I had been playing that game with him for over a year and that I assumed it meant something important to him; something that he could not express with words, so I had made it my task to try to understand his message. I said to him that I thought it must contain some anxiety about himself and about his family, something to do with his future. He replied immediately that he often thought that he would have to go to work and would not know how to do it properly and would be sacked. I asked what made him think so. He remained silent and looked sad. I said that I thought his dream made me think he feared some kind of loss or split at home and wondered if he had ever heard or thought anything that made him think that. He then said that when his parents quarrelled, his father threatened to leave. I said that I understood that part of him, at times, might want his father to leave so that he could be "the man of the family". He replied that if anything ever happened to his father, Xavier was the eldest and the one who really wanted to be the boss. I said that I thought he felt guilty about his wishes (contained in his dream), about wanting to be "the man of the family". I added that he seemed to be afraid that he would not be able to take his father's place properly (and would be sacked) because he was only a child and therefore it was easier for him to imagine that it was his brother who wanted to do those things.

He replied: "Can you teach me to make sure my house doesn't fall down?"

I said that we could both try, in the same way that we were teaching each other with the computer and the typewriter. It also occurred to me that his dream contained wishes to leave, both home and the analysis when the two situations put him under stress, but we had come to the end of the session and I felt he had had enough with what I had said to him already. I also asked myself, after he had left, if the game was a way of conveying more primitive anxieties about himself. I have not found any evidence of this so far. I thought, though, that the dream about the Pope and Fidel Castro, in the transference, also referred to us and his ambivalence about the analysis, the Pope representing João (as well as his father) and Castro standing for me.

My meeting with João's parents was due and I made arrangements to see them. Much to my regret, Mr and Mrs Y have never seen the colleague to whom I had referred them. There were all kinds of excuses for their avoidance: she lived too far away, Mr Y's schedule never allowed them to arrange a mutually convenient appointment, etc. I thought that they were afraid of facing some of their marital difficulties and, in addition, of confronting their feelings of inadequacy as parents. Mrs Y frequently wondered if it was really necessary for João to come to see me so often and, occasionally, would mumble something about how "when we were children, nobody had to send their children to the psychiatrist". I was aware of her feelings of guilt, and of exclusion from her son's relationship with me, and thought she could boycott the analysis if under threat. I now felt more certain of my initial understanding that the presence of the housekeeper and the Swiss Guard in the dream represented both his mother's and his own ambivalent feelings about me. The father, as if he could read my mind, came to my help by saying that it was important that João should continue because he was much happier and gave them less trouble at home since he had started coming here.

Our meeting took place the day after the session in which João told me about his dream with the Pope. In the course of our meeting, I raised the question that João had put in my mind the day before: had they, during their difficult moments, ever considered separation? They appeared taken aback and denied it. There was a difficult silence, which Mrs Y broke to tell me that she had never thought about it; she had married for life, she said. Raising her voice a little, she turned towards her husband and told me that he often said that when the children finished school and were ready to go to university, he would leave. "To do what, he has never explained," she added angrily. She said she did not know if their sons knew about his plans, but she would not be surprised if they did. Mr Y looked very embarrassed and I felt sorry for him. He did not seem to know what to say and I, once again, said that was the sort of thing I would have preferred them to discuss with someone else. He said that perhaps he needed to talk to someone like me. He felt that he had married very young and, being the eldest, he had always had responsibilities he had not asked for. He felt that once his children went to university, he would have his chance "to do my own thing". "And what about me then?" Mrs Y said, with tears in her eyes. He said he had never meant to leave her, only to have the freedom to come and go as he pleased without feeling compelled "to perform". (I silently wondered about sexual problems in their relationship and the possibility that João's unconscious perception of them might be contained in the "build a house" game.) He said he wanted to reassure me that their troubles would never stand in their children's way and that João would continue to come and see me "for however long it was necessary". Time was up and, reluctantly, I ended the session. As they were leaving, he turned around and said that they would make an effort to arrange an appointment "to go and see the lady you want us to see". Alas, they have not done so.

I am grateful to Abrahão Brafman for his comments on yet another way of understanding João's dream about the Pope and Fidel Castro. I should like to quote him: "I could not resist imagining that 'papá' (father) had been making many references about the 'Fidel'—the Spanish you—a fact/wish he confirms by saying he needed to speak to someone like you."

The incident involving the computer and the typewriter marked a turning point in João's analysis. His discovery of a parent/analyst, with whom he could engage in playing, learning, and teaching, gave a new character to our relationship. João found it difficult to believe that I knew nothing about computers. I found it necessary to be honest with him because of his acute sensitivity to any signs of falseness in his objects. It took him some time to accept that it was true and not a trick of mine to get at him in some way. He seemed to derive pleasure from being able to teach me something that he knew. This de-idealization of adults who are not omnipotent allowed for a reciprocity where we taught and helped each other. Those unfamiliar with the concept of "developmental help" (Edgcumbe, 2000, pp. 160–195; Gavshon, 1988; Hurry, 1998, pp. 32–73) as part of psychoanalytic technique with children may mistakenly see this as a mere counter-transference enactment. Instead, it provided João with a newly acquired confidence and the growth of a trusting and productive therapeutic alliance.

Like Segismundo (Calderón de la Barca's hero), João tries in vain to convince himself that life in his inner world is just a dream, thus attempting to avoid both disappointment and punishment in his life in the external world:

Yo sueño que estoy aquí
destas prisiones cargado,
y soñé que en otro estado
más lisonjero me vi.
¿Qué es la vida? Un frenesí.
¿Qué es la vida? Una ilusión,
una sombra, una ficción,
y el mayor bien es pequeño,
que toda la vida es sueño,
y los sueños sueños son.

[Calderón de la Barca, 1998 (1636), pp. 164–165]

(I dream that I am here
Bound down by these heavy chains
And I dreamed that once I lived differently
And was happy.
What is life? A frenzy.
Life's an illusion
Life's a shadow, a fiction,
And the greatest good is worth nothing at all,
For the whole of life is just a dream
And dreams . . . dreams are only dreams)

It is my hope that analysis will help João to come to terms with the difficulties his instinctual wishes, and the complex object-relations that they shape, will enable him to go forward to the next and more difficult developmental stage he still has to master: adolescence. Perhaps then, like Basilio (Segismundo's father), his internalized father could say to him:

Hijo—que tan noble acción
otra vez en mis entrañas
te engendra—príncipe eres
A ti el laurel y la palma
se te deben; tú venciste,
corónente tus hazañas.

[Calderón de la Barca, 1998 (1636), p. 205]

(My son, in your nobility you are reborn.[3]
You are prince; the laurel and the palm of victory
Are yours. You overcame. Your achievements
Give you victory.)

Acknowledgement

Special thanks to Pauline Cohen who patiently and in vain waited for João's parents to contact her, and to Jenny Kaplan-Davids whose comments are integrated in the thinking behind this paper. I would also like to express my gratitude to Abrahão Brafman, Sheilagh Davies, Felicity Dirmeik, Audrey Gavshon, Anne-Marie Sandler and Sharon Stekelman for their useful suggestions and comments.

Notes

1. "Experience derived from analyses—and not the theory of dreams—informs us that in children any wish left over from waking life is sufficient to call up a dream, which always emerges as connected and ingenious but usually short, and which is easily recognized as a wish fulfilment."
2. This is the accepted English translation. In fact, it changes the first line of the original, which actually says: "As life is so short".
3. The original says: "My son, in your nobility you are reborn from my entrails."

References

Calderón de la Barca, P. (1998)[1636] *La vida es sueño.* Edición de Ciriaco Morón, Madrid: Ediciones Cátedra, S.A. English translation (1998), J. Clifford (Trans.), *Life is a Dream.* London: Nick Hern Books.

Edgcumbe, R. (2000). *Anna Freud: A View of Development, Disturbance and Therapeutic Techniques.* London: Routledge.

Flanders, S. (Ed.) (1993). *The Dream Discourse Today.* London: New Library of Psychoanalysis.

Freud, A. (1927)[1974]. Four lectures on child analysis. *The Writings of Anna Freud, Volume 1* (pp. 3–69) New York: International Universities Press.

Freud, A. (1969)[1972]. Difficulties in the path of psychoanalysis: a confrontation of past with present viewpoints. In: *Problems of Psychoanalytic Technique and Theory 1966–1970* (pp. 124–156). London: Hogarth Press.

Freud, S. (1900a). The interpretation of dreams. *S.E., IV–V: ix–xii*, 1–621. London: Hogarth Press, revised edition, 1925.

Freud, S. (1905c). Jokes and their relation to the unconscious. *S.E.*, 8: 161. London: Hogarth Press.

Freud, S. (1916)[1916–1917]. Introductory lectures on psycho-analysis. *S.E., XV–XVI*: 126. London: Hogarth Press.

Gavshon, A. (1988). Playing: its role in child analysis. *Bulletin of the Anna Freud Centre*, 11(2): 128–145.

Hurry, A. (1998). *Psychoanalysis and Developmental Therapy*. London: Karnac.

Rodríguez de la Sierra, L. (1996). Is it true that children seldom report their dreams? *Psychoanalysis in Europe*, 46, Spring: 66–81.

CHAPTER SIX

On interpretation and holding

Anne-Marie Sandler

W hen I sat down to write this paper, my task turned out not to be as straightforward as I had expected. I had assumed that what is meant by "holding" was relatively clear and simple. I discovered, however, that the concept of "holding" as used in the literature covers many things and that it belongs to that class of concepts that have an "elastic" meaning space, that is to say, a meaning that changes according to the specific context in which they are employed.

There is little doubt that the analytic situation, as developed by Freud, with its constant setting, its regular hours, its somewhat ritualized external trappings, provides the patient with a feeling of safety, a sense of being held. Winnicott, in particular, was very aware of the relevance of the analytic setting to the patient, and gave special importance to it. As we all know, Winnicott (1965) introduced the term "holding environment" as a metaphor for certain aspects of the analytic situation and the analytic process. The term derives from the maternal function of holding the infant, but, taken as a metaphor, it has a much broader application and extends beyond the infantile period to the broader caretaking function of the parent. Winnicott transferred this concept to an aspect of the analyst's function, with full awareness of the analyst's capacity to exercise a caretaking role. But for Winnicott this caretaking was always more than simple support and the provision of a reliable and reassuring presence. As he once remarked, it "often takes the form of conveying in words, at the appropriate moment, something that shows that the analyst knows and understands the deepest anxiety that is being experienced, or that is waiting to be experienced".

Many of Winnicott's views on holding have their origin in some aspects of Ferenczi's (1926) ideas on "active" technique, and in the technique of Ferenczi's analytic heir, Michael Balint (1968). Both these authors were closely attuned to the way in which the analytic setting tended to exert a regressive pull on patients, facilitating the expression of primitive object relations and urges. In the same period of time, Wilfred Bion (1970) described the analyst as functioning in a maternal role, as a "container" for the patient's projections. By this, he meant that the analyst can accept the externalizations of the patient, hold them, and work over them by means of what he has called "reverie". Only then are they returned to the patient in the form of appropriate interpretations.

Another meaning "holding" can assume in the treatment of violent patients, whether children or adults, consists of setting appropriate limits or exercising restraints so that the patient feels that he will not do irreparable damage to himself or to the analyst. In this context, we should also consider relevant writings on the analyst's function in the treatment of narcissistic characters and borderline cases, and I refer here particularly to the work of Heinz Kohut (1971) and Otto Kernberg (1975). Kohut's technique, based on the notion of environmental failure in early childhood, certainly implies a major holding function in its emphasis on the communication of empathy and its associated de-emphasis on the importance of interpreting internal conflict. For Kohut the notion of deficit and the feeling states associated with it are at the centre of the analyst's concern. Kernberg's technical recommendations, on the other hand, are rather different. He argues that it is the patient's powerful envious and aggressive impulses that interfere with the integrative work of the analysis and he thus believes that a clear and firm "contract" with the patient, together with a very active and structuring interpretative stance, will hold him best. Borderline cases are often terrified of their destructive urges, and the solidity of the frame as well as frequent interpretations will, Kernberg believes, contain the patient's terror that the analyst will not be able to survive his or her assaults.

Turning now to the concept of interpretation, we find ourselves again in territory that is not as precisely defined as we would wish it to be. I am not going to refer to the numerous writings of others on this topic, except to say that the fine distinctions between interpretations, confrontations, explanations, clarifications, and the like are to my mind beyond the scope of this paper. What I do find relevant in relation to a discussion on holding and interpretation is the distinction between interpretation of what is going on in the patient in the present (including, pre-eminently, transference interpretations) on the one hand, and constructions and reconstructions on the other. In my view, constructions and reconstructions are elaborations that should normally come in the wake of immediate here-and-now interpretations. I make this distinction because I do not subscribe to the old archaeological view of psychoanalytic technique, where the aim is simply to progressively uncover the buried past. While the recovery of past memories certainly provides valuable material for reconstruction, their importance is only as great as the insight they can provide into the way the patient functions in the present.

In an attempt to formulate the task of analysis, I would say that analysis is for me much more than the sum of the patient's associations and the analyst's interpretations. While the analyst tries to understand the conscious and unconscious meaning of the patient's communications, it is equally his role as analyst to formulate appropriate parts of his understanding in such a way that it can be conveyed in the most suitable form to the patient. By suitable in this context I mean the way that takes into account the level of development on which the patient functions, the organization of his resistances, his specific vulnerabilities and anxieties, particularly his susceptibility to feelings of guilt, shame, and humiliation. Not everything that is understood can be appropriately conveyed to the patient at any given time, and what is appropriate must always be made. In this connection, issues of tact and the timing of interpretations assume a special importance.

One of the main aims of our analytic endeavour is to help child, adolescent, or adult patients to learn to tolerate the infantile wishful aspects of themselves. These infantile, often very primitive, wishes have aroused painful conflict in the individual, and have become threatening during the course of development. As a consequence they have been defended against, possibly with pathological results. We strive to get our patients to tolerate these parts of themselves in their conscious thinking and phantasies, so that they are not compelled to act them out, or to extend pathogenic efforts to keep them in check. To put it another way: a major analytic goal is to get patients to become friends with the previously unacceptable parts of themselves, to get on good terms with previously threatening wishes and phantasies. To do this means that we have to provide, through our interpretations and the way we give them, an atmosphere of tolerance of the infantile, the perverse and the ridiculous, an atmosphere that the patients can make part of their own attitudes towards themselves, which they can internalize along with the understanding they have reached in their joint work with the analyst.

Of course, when we speak of the conflictual aspects of the patient's own self we include in this the complicated, conflict-laden relationships that the child or the adult has established with his introjects. One of our central tasks is to help all our patients to become familiar with the way they interact with these introjects in their unconscious phantasy life, so that they can gradually become familiar with and accept the previously unacceptable parts of themselves, which they located in their introjects during the course of their development.

From this it follows that great importance must be given to the analysis of the patient's resistances to the analytic process. For me, this means more than pointing out the patient's use of one or other defence mechanism. It means that the analyst normally has to phrase the interpretation he or she gives in such a way that it lowers the patient's resistance to accepting what was previously unacceptable, to enable them to contain more readily what was previously repugnant to their consciousness. This requires a constant monitoring on the analyst's part of the patient's conscious and unconscious receptivity to his or her interventions.

The primary preoccupation of the analyst must, in my view, be the understanding, and appropriate communication to the patient, of what is happening in the here-and-now of the analysis. It is this type of analysis that makes, I believe, the closest contact with the patient's underlying feelings, the feelings that are most accessible or potentially accessible. I am convinced that it is by exploring the immediate current conflict existing within the analytic situation that the analyst paves the way to later necessary reconstructions of the past. What has to be listened for most carefully in our work are those elements of the patient's preoccupations that relate to the person of the analyst or to the analytic process, elements that represent transference in the broadest sense of the term. To interpret the past before the present often offers the patient the chance to escape by bypassing current resistances, in this way avoiding the experiencing of psychic pain and its exploration by distancing and intellectualization, a process that does not help the analysis. Reconstruction of the past at the appropriate time has, of course, an important role to play in that it provides a meaningful historical or biographical context for the consolidation of insight, a matrix for the anchoring of insights that have first been gained through the analysis of the patient's immediate conflicts in the here-and-now of the analysis.

It is generally accepted that the analysts' ongoing self-analysis, in particular the analysis of their counter-transference thoughts and feelings about their patients, is an important component of the analytic work. This is particularly so when we work with children and adolescents, where we are often struggling with peremptory wishes and intense conflicts that are forcefully externalized on to the person of the analyst. The patient's transference wishes, whether conscious or unconscious, involve roles for the analyst as well as for the patient, and the analyst will react to the patient's attempts to impose such roles on him or her in a variety of ways. Some of these reactions may interfere with the work arising from the side of the analyst. At these times, the analyst's self-scrutiny, to the extent that self-analysis is possible, acquires a special urgency, and may lead to the understanding of some crucial resistance in the patient.

Finally, not even in the best conducted analyses does the interpretative work proceed on a straight and narrow path. The analyst may collude, often for relatively long periods, with one or other of the patient's resistances. Moreover, the analyst will go through periods of confusion during which he or she may feel lost or may pursue an incorrect track. I do not think that this is a bad thing—indeed, I think it is inevitable. What is important is that the analyst eventually reaches a point where he or she becomes aware of what has been going on, and can then make the appropriate interpretation to the patient.

To end these introductory remarks, may I remind you that in severe disturbances it is often extremely difficult to know whether we are dealing with an arrest in development, with deficient structures, or whether we are witnessing the result of regressive and defensive manoeuvres due to unbearably painful affects linked with threatening phantasies of one sort or another. As a result, we may be tempted, on certain occasions, to try to "hold" the patient by working in the positive transference, or even by reassuring rather than interpreting. In working with children it is, of course, extremely easy to slip into a friendly, slightly educational mode. However, most frequently, an interpretation of what is going on in the here-and-now, if formulated appropriately, can relieve anxiety in patients who are so disturbed that it seems as if only the reassuring kind of "holding" could be of help. Please understand that I am not making a case for the "magic" of interpretation, although I do want to emphasize that interpretations can have widely differing effects, depending on the way they are conceived and formulated. I also feel that because of their fear of giving reassurance to the patient (which is on the whole not an appropriate measure in analysis) many analysts appear to be afraid to give interpretations that have a reassuring effect (which, in my view, is not only legitimate but also very appropriate in the analytic work). To give a correct interpretation that brings about reassurance is not the same as reassuring the patient by telling him that "things are not so bad".

In order to illustrate how difficult it often is to differentiate and to clarify what is holding and what is interpretation, I want now to give two very brief clinical vignettes from the analysis of Danny, aged six years. He was diagnosed as a child with a severe narcissistic disorder and some important borderline features. The referral was precipitated by Danny having suddenly and viciously attacked his female teacher.

When I saw the parents, Father struck me as an intelligent but very anxious man in his forties. Mother, who was substantially younger, looked pale, with large bags under her eyes. She seemed frightened, depressed, and generally bewildered. As we proceeded, it became clear that Father was the dominant member of the couple. He was very verbal, for the most part clear in what he said, though at times he became lost in a torrent of words.

From the mass of information I was given at that interview (and later) I pieced together the following story. The parents had married when Mother was still a student, and seven years passed before they decided to have a child. With Danny, they had problems from the moment of his conception. Mother was very anxious, and a troubled pregnancy was followed by a difficult delivery. Mother was horrified to discover that her baby had a very severe squint. She became convinced that he was a damaged baby, and reacted with feelings of guilt and depression. Because he had been blue at birth, and because he tended to fall asleep in the middle of his feeds, Mother insisted that he undergo intensive neurological examinations in the USA. There was no sign of any neurological abnormality, no "soft signs" indicative of minimal brain damage, yet Mother clearly continued to feel that Danny was abnormal.

When I first met the parents, the family consisted of Mother, Father, Danny, and a little brother (David), four years younger, who is the apple of Mother's eye. It seemed that Danny could be very grown-up for his age. He tended to play on his own for long periods of time. The father commented on how persistent and perfectionist Danny could be. For example, Danny would do a drawing over and over again, perhaps twenty or more times, until he got it exactly right. Getting Danny ready for school in the morning and to bed at night was difficult as, according to the parents, he was very stubborn, compulsive, and provocative. While Mother would get exasperated and lose her temper, Father would tend to cajole Danny and try to bribe him. Often when frustrated, Danny would erupt in a rage, scream, and destroy the things he was fond of.

Throughout Danny's first year, there had been tension between the parents over the correct way of handling the child. At the end of the first year, just as the Mother was thinking of weaning Danny, she had a sudden severe attack of asthma and was rushed to hospital. The breast-feeding stopped very abruptly.

On Mother's return from hospital she was told by her husband that she needed to rest and that he would look after the child. Mother felt unable to protest, but felt robbed by him of her access to Danny. By this time Danny was an extremely verbal child, dry by day but not at night, and more or less clean, except for occasional bowel accidents. The parents—particularly the father—were frightened and intimidated by his temper tantrums. Father's technique of dealing with these was to try to reason endlessly, to make promises and to strike bargains or to use evasions and a variety of deceptions in an attempt to avoid confrontations. At the age of six, Danny still sucks his bottle as soon as he comes home from school.

Difficulties in falling asleep also caused problems. Father now has to sit by Danny's bedside and tell him stories, holding his hand, while with his other hand Danny clutches his bottle. Once asleep Danny does not wake, but is wet every night. This has lately become an embarrassing problem, as his little brother David is now totally dry. Danny had reacted badly to the birth of David. He was acutely jealous and upset about Mother breast-feeding him. After David's birth, there had also been complaints that Danny was biting other children at nursery school. At present the greatest source of friction between Mother and Danny is his constant teasing and provocation of his brother, something that the mother finds intolerable.

The parents—the Mother much more than the Father—do lose their temper with Danny, and then hit him or scream at him, feeling very guilty afterwards. However, their helplessness in the face of much of his aggressive behaviour is surprising. For example, Danny has developed the habit of using what he calls "poo-talk" at table, telling his brother that what he is eating is piss or shit—"poo-sausages" or "poo-spaghetti". He also teases and frightens him by saying "Of shit you are made and to shit you will return", until finally David bursts into tears. The parents are very upset by this behaviour, but feel unable to do anything about it. Their paralysis is due both to their fear of Danny's rage and their guilt at the thought of damaging him.

The parents think that Danny is under great strain at school because he often comes home in an irritable mood, occasionally having soiled himself on the way home. Outside school he has one friend, an older child, who lives nearby. They are said to get on well together, mostly engrossed in imaginative play.

There is much more that one can say about Danny and his parents, but this provides a reasonably full picture of the child and his relation to his family. After some weeks of seeing the parents, it was agreed that I would continue to work with them once a week, and that Danny should be seen for more intensive treatment.

It was possible to arrange for a gifted trainee, Miss Smith, to see Danny on a daily basis, and for me to supervise the work. Miss Smith saw the parents briefly, and then had her first session with Danny. She reported that she had been quite taken aback by his appearance. He was small, wore large thick spectacles, had a pinched face, and his squint was very noticeable. He did not respond to Miss Smith's greeting, avoided eye contact throughout the session, remaining sullen and hiding behind Mother.

Danny had started to kick Mother on the way to the consulting room, and continued this inside the room. At first Mother tried to ignore this, but it got worse. The therapist suggested to Danny that he might inspect the toys in the room. This had no effect, so she then commented that Mother might like to look at the toys with Danny. This seemed to work, and Danny inspected the toys, without any change of expression. He did not play until he had found a gun that shot a stick with a suction pad at the end. He then shot it all over the place and hit the therapist. She said that while it was fun to play with guns, she didn't like to be hit, just as he would not like to be hit. She suggested that he find a target to shoot at. Danny accepted this, and found a small house that he placed in the sandbox, using it as his target.

It may be worth commenting that here the therapist orientated herself to the child's aggression and deflected it to a more neutral object—a minor bit of holding, perhaps. She also created a safe analytic frame for the child, clarifying that she would see to it that neither he nor she would get hurt in the consultation room. However, my own inclination would have been to see the child's behaviour as motivated by anxiety. My first preoccupation would have been to try and find some way of interpreting, either directly or via his mother, that to come to see a strange lady is perhaps very scary, and that he may be trying to show the therapist that he is the strong one who does the scaring. Addressing his anxiety in the here-and-now of the session has also, in my view, to be considered as a piece of holding.

After Danny shot at the doll's house several times, he became very excited, shouting "I'll break you all up". He managed to raise clouds of sand, but then looked for something that would serve as a fortification to protect the house. He first used fences, which he blew up, shrieking with excitement and passing wind. He then found a large elephant that he placed in front of the house. This time no amount of shooting could move the elephant. Danny became furious, shouting at the elephant that it was arrogant, stubborn, and impertinent and that he would destroy it and teach it a lesson. "I'll show you, I'll show you", he screamed. Danny, in his excitement, now began to throw handfuls of sand and toys about the room.

Miss Smith commented at this point, which was towards the end of the session, that she understood that Danny felt furious and humiliated that the elephant was so strong, because that made him feel rather small and weak. Danny did react to this by quietening down, although he went on shooting viciously at the elephant's belly.

Danny's behaviour could be understood in a number of ways. The therapist chose to comment on Danny's anger and likely humiliation, hoping that by naming the possible conflict the child would feel helped and understood. Certainly her intervention had a quietening effect. From the material of this session, however, many of us may have been inclined to see in the shooting of the elephant a representation of Danny's aggressive phantasies towards Mother's pregnancy. For some, the house may have appeared to allude to a phantasy of a home that seems very unsafe and that Danny tries to protect. The sense of excitement, which accompanied Danny's play, seemed to point to very eroticized phantasies, particularly with anal eroticism. We are then faced with the question of whether to interpret and what to interpret in order to reduce anxiety or limit aggression. It seems often very useful to reflect on why a patient brought a specific piece of material in a given session because it may help the analyst to get orientated in order to best interpret and hold the patient.

In this sequence of his play, Danny, having expressed the wish to break up the house, used the elephant as a fortification to protect it. He accuses the elephant of being arrogant, stubborn, and impertinent and declares that the elephant needs to be taught a lesson. These accusations reflect those of his mother towards him. Do we not have to presume that he would be quite scared at being brought to a strange lady for therapy even if the parents took great pains to explain why he was coming? Could one then ask oneself whether one aspect of the material could be Danny's attempt to actualize in the session an unconscious super-ego scenario, a scenario between the primitive punitive demands of his conscience and his belea-guered ego, which expects severe retributions? Could his anxieties in this very first session be linked with his fear of an attack from the therapist, possibly an attack in the form of punishment for his misdeeds? If we believe this, an interpretation of the child's anxiety, preferably linked with the therapist in the here-and-now of the session would, in my view, have been more appropriate.

> That the therapist was seen as a terrifying aggressor was borne out by a drawing that Danny made in his next session. It depicted a terrible monster, with human features, many limbs and sharp teeth. The monster had a clock in its belly, with the hands pointing to ten minutes before the hour. He referred to the clock as a bomb. Danny's vision of the therapist as a frightening monster seems to be the result of the externalization of his reproaching super-ego, which Danny experiences as an internal attacker. Danny gets rid of the guilty or shameful aspects of his own self by projection—the therapist is the villain—while simul-taneously identifying with a powerful internal figure, thus attaining a double gain in his internal dynamics.

> It took Danny some weeks to allow Mother to leave the treatment room. Increasingly, he directed the sessions by insisting that he and Miss Smith play football. He would come in like a tornado, carrying his own football, neither greeting nor looking at the therapist, and would immediately clear a space for the game. He would then proceed to show how proficient he was at kicking and dribbling the ball. He constantly tried to teach Miss Smith in a very didactic way. He kept count of the score meticulously from session to session, but had his own system of awarding points, so that he very soon became the undis-puted winner far, far ahead of the therapist. He drew provocative pictures of the mocking winner and the disconsolate loser.

> This obsessive and repetitive play could not be checked for several weeks, but finally Miss Smith managed to reach an agreement that the last twenty minutes or so of the session should be spent more quietly. Danny accepted this, and they started to play board games—draughts, snakes and ladders and chess. Here again, Danny, as might be expected, was constantly critical and scornful of Miss Smith and would interrupt the game when there was any danger of his losing.

> The games provided, however, an opportunity for conversation, and Danny gradually became more relaxed, able to call his therapist by her name and to make eye contact with her. The football game became less

compulsive, and was replaced by the enactment of endless battles involving toy cars, animals, soldiers, and space invaders. Miss Smith was invariably the enemy and the conflict was always over the possession of territory. Naturally the therapist was the loser, and a negotiated peace was never possible.

Miss Smith and I puzzled over Danny's repeated phantasies of conquering and possessing, invariably accompanied by the danger of being attacked, threatened, and tricked by vicious enemies. We came to believe that this represented his rather frantic attempt to find a solution to his opposing wishes for distance and closeness. On the one hand, he tried to deny his need of and his dependency on his objects and at times behaved as if he was an all powerful, fiercely independent adult. At other times, however, he seemed to merge with the therapist, not allowing her a mind or a will of her own, expecting her to mirror his wishes and needs. Danny seemed not to live in a triangulated Oedipal space but appeared to be caught in a dyadic relation, with no one to mediate his anxieties linked with his greedy and aggressive urges. We were witnessing his struggle to control and dominate and his fears of retribution and punishment. However, very gradually Miss Smith was allowed to become less representative of a persecuting introject, more of a friend and ally, and for increasing periods of time Danny could relax his early rigid control. This progress was most probably due to the combined effect of the therapist's interpretations and of her presence as a consistently reliable, interested, and thinking object.

After some months of therapy, Danny started to show signs of increasing upset at the end of sessions, at weekends and before holidays. He tended to react aggressively at these times, yet strenuously deny that he cared about the therapist or that he minded the separation. Danny appeared particularly to experience the ending of the sessions as an attack, as a reminder of the inequality between him and the therapist who kept the analytic frame and whom he could not control. This seemed to make him feel unbearably vulnerable.

The session I wish to describe in detail was largely peaceful and friendly. Danny had been singing while making a cannon with building materials. He had allowed the therapist to be helpful and was proud of his achievement. A few minutes before the end of the session, the therapist warned him that it would soon be time to clear up and that she would help him move the cannon into his cupboard. Danny became contrary, managed to break a part of the cannon and insisted that she had broken it. When the therapist had to remind him once more that the time was up, Danny lost control and threw everything that he could lay his hands on around the room, making a considerable amount of noise in the process. Father, who heard this, came to the consulting room and, despite the therapist's efforts to keep him out, insisted that he and Danny were going to clear up the mess. As soon as he could, Danny escaped Father's grip and rushed out without another look.

When Danny came back after the weekend break, he entered the room like a tornado, accusing Miss Smith of not having got the room ready for him. He kicked her, tried to bite her and managed to scratch her face, drawing blood. She had no choice but to hold him down while saying to him that she would not let him hurt himself or her, because it would make him feel unsafe. Danny started to scream to drown her voice, and struggled to get free. The commotion brought Mother to the office. The therapist asked Danny whether he thought he could quieten down or whether he preferred to go home. She repeated that she could see how upset and angry he was, but that she could not let him hurt her. She was attempting to re-establish a safer environment, one in which Danny would feel sufficiently held. Danny's only reaction was to scream louder and to try to hit out. He finally managed to wriggle free from the therapist's hold but knocked his lip, which started to bleed. This seemed to increase Danny's panic. He refused to leave the room and lay on the floor kicking, swearing and crying. Finally, Mother bribed Danny with the promise of a treat and he rushed out of the treatment room.

Certainly the way this session began reflected a situation in which physical restraint was necessary—a literal "holding" —for the protection of both the therapist and the patient. And yet we are faced here with a real difficulty. How can we decide whether Danny's behaviour is best understood as an outburst of uncontained aggression in an impulsive child or whether his violence is the direct result of a panic state in a borderline child whose narcissism has been challenged, especially as he had started to relinquish some of his omnipotent control? But, whatever understanding the therapist may come to, the need, first and foremost, to create a safe environment for the child was paramount. It may be useful to recall here Kernberg's remark that borderline patients are often terrified of their destructive urges and the consequent destruction of their objects.

The end of Friday's session had seemed unbearable to Danny. Being on the threshold of relating to his therapist in a less controlling way, he had become more vulnerable with regard to his wishes and desires towards her. The long weekend ahead plunged Danny into an acutely painful state of helplessness. This had been enhanced by Father's intrusion in the treatment room. As a result Danny's sense of humiliation and offence had felt overwhelming. His rage and indignation towards his therapist, whom, he felt, had betrayed him, was intense. He appeared to express it clearly in his accusation, as he entered the consulting room: "You don't have the room ready for me." It was as if Danny had to prove to himself that she had forgotten him, that she had let him down.

In this perspective a distinction is made between basic aggressive urges, which can erupt if the ego's control is too weak—as seen in what Fenichel (1945) described as impulse-ridden characters—and defensively aggressive behaviour of the sort that I believe was repeatedly shown by Danny. This type of reaction, in which there is a sudden outburst of uncontrollable anger, coupled with accusations, is so common that it deserves special attention, particularly with regard to the challenge it poses to the therapist. Most frequently interpretations or psychological "holding" go by the board in the immediate response to an outburst of narcissistic rage. Literal holding is often the only way to protect both the child and the therapist.

In cases like Danny's, where the child experienced a state of overwhelming helplessness and disintegration, the content of the accusations invariably reflects the content of the internal accusations towards an unsafe, deeply frightening, and shaming world. Having been able to show the child that the therapist does survive the outbursts and does not retaliate, interpretative work on the patient's phantasies can then be usefully made. They will be part of the holding function of the analytic process.

It seems important to add that the eruption of the parents into the treatment room seemed to indicate their inability to contain their own anxiety and to trust the therapist to cope with Danny. It also shows how they tended to project on their son their inner representation of him as a dangerous, violent, and destructive child.

I have presented these vignettes in an effort to illustrate the complexity of the analytic task with children. The reader may like to know that after a year and a half of treatment, Danny has shown some improvement. At school he performs exceedingly well and is one of the teachers' favourite pupils. He is regarded as reliable. At home things are somewhat better. He is mostly dry at night and the soiling has completely disappeared. He is said to be rather more cooperative and the parents have reported that there are moments when Danny looks happy. He is also physically more affectionate towards Mother, which he had not been previously. The food fads are still there and he regresses easily to his previous way of functioning when he feels too bad about himself. Recently he has decided, of his own accord, to give up his bottle and he is proud of and relieved by this.

In this paper, I have tried to discuss and illustrate some of the meanings of holding and interpretation. In the work with Danny, I have attempted to illustrate how, as an analyst, one is constantly reflecting on the various meanings of the child's material, on the state of the transference and counter-transference in the here-and-now of the session, on the child's basic defensive modes and fluctuating affective states. As we understand some aspects of a child's material, we tend to interpret what we think has been going on, in order to give to the child a shared sense of what has occurred in the session. Often it is then possible to make links with other situations in the child's life. We try to assess the effect of our interpretations in order to help the child sustain further insights. By attempting to help the patient to become acquainted with aspects of his or her personality, aspects that were kept out of consciousness, the analyst can often be felt by the child to be a threatening and dangerous person. After all, these repudiated unconscious wishes have been rejected, defended against in the course of development, in an attempt to maintain what felt at the time to be the best possible equilibrium. Thus, in the course of an analysis, we expect patients to reorganize that equilibrium. If children do accept and take in our interpretations, a gradual change is bound to occur. That is to say that children, by accepting little by little the new insights given to them, learn to tolerate certain infantile, wishful aspects of themselves, which they would have preferred to ignore. In the view presented here, this acceptance can only occur in an atmosphere of tolerance of the infantile, of the often perverse, contradictory, violent, and bizarre aspects of our unconscious mind. This atmosphere of tolerance represents, in my view, an important kind of holding.

I would like to put forward the idea that patients do perceive, in the course of treatment, the complexity of the analytic work. Alongside the verbal communications, the patients do witness in their analyst an attitude of special and consistent interest, a recognition of their being remembered in their uniqueness. Patients do pick up the analyst's interest and willingness to reflect on feelings and behaviour, and gain a strong sense that they are being held in mind. This awareness is, of course, always threatened and often lost through a variety of destructive attacks, but the regularity of the sessions and the consistent presence, concern, and attitude of the analyst represents the holding aspect of any psychoanalytic treatment, a holding aspect that is necessary to allow for productive interpretative work. Thus, in conclusion, I am led to propose that holding is a basic ingredient, a quality intrinsic to any therapeutic endeavour and that it does not seem to be helpful to try and oppose interpretation and holding.

Acknowledgement

I should like to express my sincere gratitude to Miss Smith who so generously provided me with the treatment material which formed the main part of this paper.

References

Balint, M. (1968). *The Basic Fault*. London: Tavistock.
Bion, W. (1970). *Learning From Experience*. London: Heinemann.
Fenichel, O. (1945). *The Psychoanalytic Theory of Neurosis*. New York: Norton.
Ferenczi, S. (1926). *Further Contributions to the Theory and Technique of Psychoanalysis*. London: Hogarth.
Kernberg, O. F. (1975). *Borderline Conditions and Pathological Narcissism*. New York: Jason Aronson.

Kohut, H. (1971). *The Analysis of the Self*. New York: International Universities Press.

Winnicott, D. W. (1965). *The Maturational Processes and the Facilitating Environment*. New York: International Universities Press.

INDEX